The Sunnier Side of DOUBT

Other books by Alister McGrath:

Explaining Your Faith, Zondervan, 1989

The Intellectual Origins of the European Reformation, Basil Blackwood, 1988

Iustitia Dei: A History of the Christian Doctrine of Justification 2 vols., Cambridge University Press, 1986

Justification by Faith, Zondervan, 1988

Luther's Theology of the Cross, Basil Blackwell, 1985

The Making of Modern German Christology: From the Enlightenment to Pannenberg, Basil Blackwell, 1988

The Mystery of the Cross, Zondervan, 1988

Reformation Thought, Basil Blackwell, 1988

Understanding Jesus: Who Jesus Christ Is and Why He Matters, Zondervan, 1987

Understanding the Trinity, Zondervan, 1988

The Sunnier Side of DOUBT

ALISTER E. McGRATH

Academie Books
Grand Rapids, Michigan
Zondervan Publishing House

The Sunnier Side of Doubt
Copyright © 1990 by Alister E. McGrath

Academie Books is an imprint of Zondervan Publishing House,
1415 Lake Drive, S.E., Grand Rapids, Michigan 49506.

Library of Congress Cataloging in Publication Data

McGrath, Alister E., 1953-
 The sunnier side of doubt : what it is, how to handle it, when to value
 it, why it deepens our faith /
 Alister E. McGrath.
     p.   cm.
   Includes bibliographical references.
   ISBN 0-310-29661-7
   1. Faith.   I. Title.
 BT774.M33   1990
 234'.2—dc20   89-77250
                                                                CIP

Edited by Jan M. Ortiz
Designed by Jan M. Ortiz

Printed in the United States of America

90 91 92 93 94 95 / CH / 10 9 8 7 6 5 4 3 2 1

Contents

Preface

"Lord, I believe! Help my unbelief!" (Mark 9:24 KJV). We don't know the name of the man who spoke these memorable words to Jesus. Whoever he was, his words capture perfectly the anxieties of many Christians. They have discovered in Jesus Christ something far more wonderful than they had ever dared to hope. God often seems very close in the first days of faith. Yet nagging doubts sometimes remain. Can I really trust in the gospel? Surely it's just too good to be true! Does God really love me? Can I be of any use to God? Deep down, many Christians worry about questions like these, often feeling ashamed for doing so. And so they suppress them. They hope that they will go away. Sometimes they do—but often they don't.

This book explains what doubt is, and how it arises. It deals with a series of very specific doubts and anxieties that Christians experience, often in the first few years of their lives as believers. It offers suggestions for handling doubt, and making your faith less vulnerable to it. Its main theme is simple: Doubt is an invitation to grow in faith and understanding, rather than something we need to panic about or get preoccupied with! We must all learn to grasp and value the "sunnier side of doubt" (Tennyson).

This work had its origins in some talks given to students from Oxford University at a houseparty at Charney Manor, Oxfordshire, in December 1988. Special thanks to Emma Brining, Catherine Davis, Gillian Russell and David Stone for invaluable help in rewriting the material.

Alister McGrath

Doubt: what it is

Chapter 1

Doubt: what it is

A surprisingly large number of Christians prefer not to talk about doubt. Some even refuse to think about it. Somehow, admitting to doubt seems to amount to insulting God, calling his integrity into question. It is quite understandable that you should feel this way about doubt: on the one hand, you may feel that admitting to doubt is a sign of spiritual or intellectual weakness; on the other, you may be reluctant to admit those doubts to your friends, in case you upset them, perhaps damaging their faith.

Many Christians thus suppress their doubts, feeling that it is improper to admit them. They are afraid that they will look stupid if they do. They feel that their pride or self-esteem would suffer. Yet one of the reasons why some Christians have difficulty in coping with doubt is that they confuse it with two quite separate ideas which at first seem similar, but are actually rather different. In the first place, it's not *skepticism*—the decision to doubt everything deliberately, as a matter of principle. In the second, it's not *unbelief*—the decision not to have faith in God. Unbelief is an act of will, rather than a difficulty in understanding. Doubt often means asking questions or voicing uncertainties from the standpoint of faith. You believe—but you have difficulties with that faith, or are worried about it in some way. Faith and doubt aren't mutually exclusive— but faith and unbelief are.

Doubt is probably a permanent feature of the Christian life. It's like some kind of spiritual growing pain. Sometimes, it recedes into the background; at other times it comes to the fore, making its presence felt with a vengeance. A physician once remarked that life was a permanent battle against all sorts of diseases, with good health being little more than an ability to keep disease at bay. In many ways, the life of faith has the same shape: a permanent battle against doubt. It is helpful to think of doubt as a symptom of our human frailty, of our reluctance to trust God. Let's develop this by thinking about how people come to faith.

Coming to faith—with unresolved doubts

One way of understanding conversion runs like this. What stops people from coming to faith in God is doubt. After wrestling with these various doubts and overcoming them, the way is clear to come to faith. Coming to faith thus happens once all doubt has been cleared out of the way. Faith excludes doubt! Now it is quite possible that some people do come to faith this way. However, most do not. Experience suggests that a rather different way of understanding conversion is more reliable.

Many people feel deeply attracted by the gospel,

despite their doubts. On the one hand, their doubts are real, and hold them back from faith; on the other, the pull of the gospel is very strong, and draws them toward faith. In the end, they decide to put their trust in God and in Jesus Christ, despite unresolved anxieties and difficulties. They are still in two minds. They hope that their doubts and difficulties will be sorted out as they grow in faith. The seventeenth-century philosopher Francis Bacon commended this way in his *Advancement of Learning*: "If a man will begin with certainties, he will end in doubts; but if he is content to begin with doubts, he will end in certainties."

An analogy may make this clearer. Suppose you are at a really boring party one evening when you meet someone you feel drawn to. You get to know this person, and, as time goes on, realize you're falling in love. However, you hold back from allowing the relationship to develop any further. After all, you don't really *know* the other person that well. There might be some dark side to their character. Can you really trust them? And, like many people, you may have a sense of personal inadequacy: what, you wonder, could this other person possibly see in you? Could they ever possibly fall in love with you? You are profoundly attracted to them, yet you hold back. You have doubts. You're in two minds about it.

Now in this situation you have two options. You can still hold back and become a prisoner of your doubts and hesitations. If we all did that all the time, we'd miss out on many of life's great adventures and surprises—including both falling in love and discovering the Christian faith. Or you can take a risk. You can say, "I'm going to give this a try, and hope that my doubts and anxieties will be relieved as things go on." And so you allow the relationship to develop.

Many people become Christians in that kind of spirit. They are aware of the enormous attraction of the gospel; they are deeply moved by the thought of Jesus Christ dying for their sins; they are excited by the great gospel promises of forgiveness and newness of life. They decide to reach out in faith and claim these as their own. As for their doubts and anxieties? They hope that they will be resolved and be put in their proper perspective as their relationship with God develops. "Lord, I believe! Help my unbelief!" (Mark 9:24 KJV).

If you're in this situation, wrestling with doubt will be an important part of your life as a Christian. The way in which you came to faith sets an agenda for you. It decides what things need to be sorted out. You'll want to think about the same kind of questions that arise in any personal relationship. Can I really trust God? Does he really love me? What about my personal inadequacies—does he know what I'm *really* like? And there may be other doubts about the gospel, about yourself, about Jesus Christ, and about God himself. This book aims to deal with that agenda. *But your doubts in no way invalidate your conversion experience—you really are a Christian!*

Doubt—a reminder of human sinfulness and frailty

The gospel is about redemption. We have been set free from sin through the death and resurrection of Jesus Christ. Redemption, however, is not something that can be achieved in an instant! The story is told of a little girl who asked a bishop whether he was saved. "I have been saved from the penalty of sin, I am being saved from the

14

power of sin, and one day I shall be saved from the presence of sin," he replied. Salvation takes time! It is a process, in which we mature in faith, like a seed growing into a plant. In classic evangelical thought, a useful distinction is made between *justification* and *sanctification*. In justification, we are declared to be right with God; our status changes, as we become an adopted child of God; we are given the gift of the Holy Spirit as a surety or pledge of being a Christian. Sanctification, however, is a long process, in which we are gradually conformed to the likeness of Christ. It cannot happen overnight. The fact that it takes so long does not point to any failing on God's part, but indicates how deep-rooted sin is within us.

Martin Luther used a phrase which is very helpful here. He talked of the Christian as being "righteous and sinful at one and the same time (*simul iustus et peccator*)". By this he meant that the Christian is righteous in so far as he or she stands in a right relationship with God, but sinful in that sin has yet to be eradicated from our nature. To use a military analogy, the decisive victory over sin has been achieved with your conversion; nevertheless, mopping-up operations must continue, as isolated pockets of resistance are overcome. We are deluding ourselves if we pretend that we have no sin (1 John 1:8; 2:1). Ignoring sin, or pretending it's not there, points to an inadequate understanding of the seriousness of human sinfulness. For Paul, grace and sin are like two powers, battling it out within us. We know what the final outcome of that battle will be—but while it lasts, we cannot ignore its effects. One of those effects is doubt.

Doubt reflects the continued presence and power of

sin within us, reminding us of our need for grace and preventing us from becoming complacent about our relationship with God. We are *all* sinners, and we *all* suffer from doubt to a greater or lesser extent. Our relationship with God is something we need to work at, conscious that in doing so we are working with God and not on our own (Philippians 2:12–13). Sin causes us to challenge the promises of God, to mistrust him. (Note how mistrust of God is the "original sin" of Genesis 3:1–5). Only by causing us to turn away from God can sin regain its hold over us. Faith is not just a willingness and ability to trust in God—it is the channel through which his grace flows to us. It is our lifeline to God. It is like the trunk of a tree, transferring life-giving sap from its roots to its branches—it both supports and nourishes their growth. Break that link, and the branches wither (cf. John 15:1–8). If sin has any strategy after your conversion, it is to break that link, to deny you access to the promises and power of God—to allow itself to regain its former hold over your life.

Doubt, then, needs to be seen in its proper context— that of a struggle against sin (Hebrew 12:4). It is not an isolated phenomenon, but something that is part and parcel of the process of growing in faith and encountering resistance from our old natures in doing so.

It is not entirely correct, however, to describe doubt as simply due to human sinfulness. It is also a reflection of human *frailty*. The severe limitations placed upon human capacities by the fact that we are creatures, not God, has been a major theme of Christian theology throughout the centuries. Protesting against slick and too-easy notions of God in the fifth century, Augustine wrote of the inability of the human mind to comprehend

God fully. If you *can* comprehend it, he remarked, it's not God. Thomas Aquinas, writing in the thirteenth century, stressed that God was obliged to speak to us using images and analogies. Why? On account of the weakness of our intellects. Our minds aren't big enough to comprehend God. We cannot fully understand God and his ways: as a result, God reveals himself partially (but *accurately and adequately*), up to the limits of our abilities. This reflects a limitation on our part, not God's. Similarly John Calvin, writing in the sixteenth century, formulated his famous maxim: "God accommodates himself to our weakness." In other words, God *knows* our limitations, and adapts himself accordingly. We cannot see the full picture, so God presents us with a reliable guide to its contents, hitting the high points. No more is possible, given the limitations placed upon us. Of course we have difficulties in trying to understand God and the world—but this doesn't mean that our faith is misplaced!

An example of how human weakness affects the way we see things may help make this point clearer. Suppose you want to see the stars, or catch a glimpse of the Milky Way. You can't do this in broad daylight. You have to wait until it's dark. Now the stars are still there during the day: it's just that you can't see them. Our eyes just aren't discerning enough to pick up their light during the day. When it's night, our eyes adjust to allow us to see their tiny pinpoints of light, coming from the depths of our universe, highlighted against the blackness of the night. *The stars* don't need darkness to exist—but *we* need darkness if we are to see them, and convince ourselves that they exist! So it is with God. Just as our eyes can't see stars during the day, so our minds can't take in the fullness of God. It's the way we see things, rather than the way things actually are, which is the problem. Being human places limits on what we can see, know, and understand. Being prepared to accept these limitations is an essential part of growing in faith.

It is only natural that we should want to see and know more. But that's like wanting to see stars in the daytime! It's overlooking our limitations. It's like saying, "Because I can't see the stars in the daylight, they're not really there." That's confusing our *perception* of the situation with the *reality* of the situation! The way we see things isn't necessarily the way things really are! Doubt often reflects a sense of unease about the way in which experience, reason, feeling, and faith relate. Sometimes they seem to be out of step with each other—so which do we believe? Which is right? The central insight here is that our frailty and weakness prevent us from fully comprehending the way in which these relate to each other. As George MacDonald helpfully pointed out, "everything difficult indicates something more than our theory of life yet embraces." Faith assures us that, though we do not see the picture *totally*, we nevertheless see it *reliably* (1 Corinthians 13:12).

The vain search for certainty

Deep within all of us is a longing for absolute security, to be able to know with absolute certainty. Yet absolute certainty is reserved for a very small class of beliefs. What sort of beliefs? Well, for example, things that are self-evident or capable of being logically demonstrated by propositions. Christianity does not

18

concern logical propositions or self-evident truths (such as 2 + 2 = 4, or "the whole is greater than the part"). We may be able to know such truths with absolute certainty—but what is their relevance to life? Realizing that "the whole is greater than the part" isn't going to turn your life inside out! Knowing that two plus two equal four isn't going to tell you anything much about the meaning of life. It won't *excite* you. Frankly, the sort of things that you *can* know with absolute certainty are actually not that important.

Tennyson made this point perfectly in *The Ancient Sage*.

> For nothing worthy proving can be proven,
>   Nor yet disproven; wherefore thou be wise,
>   Cleave ever to the sunnier side of doubt.

The beliefs that are really important in life concern such things as whether there is a God and what he is like, or the mystery of human nature and destiny. These—and a whole host of other important beliefs—have two basic features. In the first place, they are *relevant* to life. They *matter*, in that they affect the way in which we think, live, hope, and act. In the second place, they cannot be *proved* or *disproved* with total certainty. By their very nature, they make claims which mean they cannot be known with absolute certainty. At best, we may hope to know them as *probably* true. There will always be an element of doubt in any statement that goes beyond the world of logic and self-evident propositions. Christianity shares this situation. It is not unique in this respect: an atheist or Marxist is confronted with precisely the same dilemma. Anyone who wants to talk about the meaning of life has to make statements which rest on faith, not absolute certainty. Anyway, God isn't a proposition—he's a person!

We cannot see God; we cannot touch him; we cannot demand that he gives a public demonstration of his existence or character. We know of God only through faith. Yet the human mind wants more. "Give us a sign! Prove it!" It is an age-old problem. Those who heard Jesus' teaching wanted a sign (Matthew 12:38)—something that would confirm his authority, that would convince them beyond any doubt.

To believe in God demands an act of faith—as does the decision not to believe in him. Neither are based upon absolute certainty, nor can they be. To accept Jesus demands a leap of faith—so does the decision to reject him. To accept Christianity demands faith—so does the decision to reject it. Both rest upon faith. Nobody can prove with absolute certainty that Jesus *is* the Son of God, the risen savior of humanity—just as nobody can prove with absolute certainty that he is *not*. The decision, whatever it may be, rests upon faith. There is an element of doubt in each case. Every attitude to Jesus—except the decision not to have any attitude at all!—rests upon faith, not certainty.

This point is made rather well by the American writer Sheldon Vanauken, who describes his mental wrestling before his conversion at Oxford as follows:

> There is a gap between the probable and the proved. How was I to cross it? If I were to stake my whole life on the risen Christ, I wanted proof. I wanted certainty. I wanted to see him eat a bit of fish. I wanted letters of fire across the sky. I got none of these. . .It was a question of whether I was to accept him—*or reject*. My God! There was a gap *behind* me as well! Perhaps the leap to acceptance was a horrifying gamble—but

what of the leap to rejection? There might be no certainty that Christ was God—but, by God, there was no certainty that he was not. This was not to be borne. I could not reject Jesus. There was only one thing to do once I had seen the gap behind me. I turned away from it, and flung myself over the gap toward Jesus.

There is indeed a leap of faith involved in Christianity but, the Christian experience is that of being caught safely by a loving and living God, whose arms await us as we leap. Martin Luther put this rather well: "Faith is a free surrender and a joyous wager on the unseen, untried and unknown goodness of God."

All outlooks on life, all theories of the meaning of human existence, rest upon faith in that they cannot be proved with absolute certainty. But this doesn't mean that they're all equally probable or plausible! Let's take three theories of the significance of Jesus to illustrate this point.

- We have been redeemed from sin by the death and resurrection of Jesus Christ.
- Jesus and his disciples were actually the advance guard of a Martian invasion force, who mistook earth for the planet Venus on account of a navigation error.
- Jesus was not so much a person as a hallucinogenic mushroom.

Although none of these can be proved or disproved with absolute certainty, it will be obvious that they cannot all be taken with quite the same degree of seriousness!

Nobody can prove Christianity with total certainty. But that's not a problem. The big questions concern the reliability of its historical foundations, its internal consistency, its rationality, its power to convert, and its relevance to human existence. As C. S. Lewis stressed in *Mere Christianity*, Christianity has exceptionally fine credentials on all counts. Look into them. You can totally commit yourself to the gospel in full confidence, as a powerful, credible and profoundly satisfying answer to the mystery of human existence. Faith is basically the resolve to live our lives on the assumption that certain things are true and trustworthy, in the confident assurance that they *are* true and trustworthy, and that one day we shall *know* with absolute certainty that they are true and trustworthy.

A superficial faith is a vulnerable faith

Superficiality is a curse of the twentieth century. The demand for instant satisfaction leads to superficial personal relationships and a superficial Christian faith. Many students discover Christianity for the first time while at college or university. This discovery very often happens alongside other important events like leaving the parental home, falling in love, or gaining independence of thought and action. As a result, initial emphasis very often falls on the emotional and experiential aspects of Christianity. There is nothing wrong with this! Christianity has abundant resources for those who wish to place emphasis on the role of experience in the life of faith. But there is more to faith than that.

Faith has three main elements. In the first place, it is *trust* in God. It is a confidence in the trustworthiness, fidelity and reliability of God. It is about rejoicing in his presence and power, being open to his prompting and guidance through prayer, and experiencing the motivation and comfort of the Holy Spirit. It is a deep sense of longing to be close to God, of wanting to praise his

22

name, of being aware of his presence. In many ways, this aspect of Christian faith is like being in love with someone: you want to be with them, enjoying their presence and feeling secure with them. It concerns the heart, rather than the head; it is emotional, rather than intellectual. It is the powerhouse of Christian life, keeping us going through the difficult times and exciting us during the good times.

The difficulty is that all too many people seem to get no further than this stage. Their faith can easily become nothing more than emotion. It can become superficial, lacking any real depth. It seems shallow. It has not really taken root, and is very vulnerable. Yet faith can only flourish when it sinks deep roots. There is more to faith than emotion, experience, and feelings, however important they may be to you. Christianity isn't just about experiencing God—it's about sticking to God. A mature faith is something secure, something that you can rely on. If your faith is not deeply rooted, you will be tempted to find security in something else, only to find that this alternative will fail you (Matthew 7:24–27).

In the second place, faith is *understanding* more about God, Jesus Christ, and human nature and destiny. By its very nature, faith seeks understanding. It seeks to take root in our minds as we think through the implications of our experience of the risen Christ. To become a Christian is to encounter the reality of God; to become a disciple is to allow this encounter to shape the way in which we think—and act. In the third place, faith is *obedience*. Paul speaks of the "obedience that comes from faith" (Romans 1:5), making the point that faith must express itself in the way we act. "Faith is kept

23

alive in us, and gathers strength, from practice more than speculation" (Joseph Addison). Perhaps one of the most practical of the New Testament letters is that written by James. Throughout this letter, we find the same point being stressed time and time again (e.g., James 2:14–26): Real faith expresses itself in works. We must not remain content with hearing the Word of God; we must allow it to affect the way in which we behave (James 1:22–25).

Part of our responsibility as Christians is to think through the consequences of our faith for the way in which we think and behave. This does not for one moment mean that every Christian should take a university degree in theology, or start working through textbooks of Christian ethics! Rather, it means allowing our faith to take root in every aspect of our lives. Notice how the New Testament letters take it for granted that their readers believe in Jesus: their concern is with deepening their understanding of that faith, and explaining what it means for our relationships with other Christians and those outside the Christian community. You must be able to explain your faith to others, who may be interested in learning what you believe and why (1 Peter 3:15). If you have not thought through what you believe—and why!—you will find this impossible.

And it's at this point that doubt can come in, simply because you have allowed your faith to be shallow. The New Testament often compares faith to a growing plant—a very helpful model to which we shall return frequently in this book. It is very easy to uproot a plant in its early stages of growth; once it has laid down roots, however, it is much harder to dislodge it. By failing to allow their faith to take root, some Christians make themselves very vulnerable to doubt. They haven't *thought* about their faith. For example, someone may raise a question about the historical evidence for the existence of Jesus. They don't know the answer. So doubts begin to creep in—often quite needless doubts, it must be said.

If this happens to you, view it in the right way. The gospel isn't an illusion which is shown up for what it really is by hard questions—like the emperor's clothes in the famous story by Hans Christian Andersen. The fact that you haven't been able to give adequate answers to some person's questions or objections to your faith doesn't mean that Christianity falls to pieces the moment people start asking hard questions! It doesn't mean that you've committed some kind of intellectual suicide by becoming a Christian. It shouldn't mean that your confidence and trust in the gospel collapse like a deflating balloon just because someone asked you a question you couldn't answer! It does, however, mean that you haven't thought these things through. Your faith is real but it is also shallow and superficial. The deficiency lies not in the gospel, but in the nature and depth of your response to it. You have allowed the gospel to capture your imagination, but not your mind. Your faith is shallow, when it should be—*and can be*—profound. Your failure here ought to be a challenge to you to go away and read more deeply about these matters, or talk them over with other more experienced Christians. In addition to helping you deepen your understanding of these things, doing this will enable you to be more helpful to those interested in learning about Christianity! This doesn't mean that you should try harder to believe, as if it were by wishing harder that difficulties disappear! Rather, it means that you should see doubt as pointing to your faith being based on weak foundations. It is those foundations which need attention. A superficial faith is a vulnerable faith, easily (and needlessly) upset when confronted with questions or criticism.

Faith is like reinforced concrete. Concrete that is reinforced with a steel framework is able to stand far greater stress and strain than concrete on its own. Experience that is reinforced with understanding will not crumble easily under pressure. Again, faith is like the flesh and bones of a human body. Just as the human skeleton supports the flesh, giving it shape and strength, so understanding supports and gives shape to Christian experience. Without the skeleton, the human body would collapse into a floppy mass. Without flesh, a skeleton is lifeless, hollow and empty; without the skeleton, flesh lacks support, form and shape. Both flesh and bones are needed if the body is to grow and to function properly. Faith needs the vitality of experience if it is to *live*. It needs the support of understanding if it is to *survive*. So reinforce your faith with understanding!

At college or university, you spend a considerable amount of time immersed in the study of your chosen subjects. Try to spend some time studying your faith as well! Read some works, such as those suggested at the end of this book, which will help you deepen your understanding of your faith. After all, the Christian students of today are the Christian leaders of tomorrow.

Doubt and individuality

We're all different. People sometimes talk about different "personalities" or "personality types." This can be helpful, up to a point: for example, some people place emphasis on understanding, while others place that emphasis on experiencing. The idea of a "personality," however, suggests that individuals are static, and doesn't pay enough attention to the fact that we change and develop in response to situations. What we are like is affected by the situations we've been through. Part of the reason that we're all different is that we've been through different situations. Who you are and the experiences you've been through can have a quite definite effect on the anxieties and doubts you have in relation to your Christian faith. Some examples will help make this point clearer.

Ann had a very difficult relationship with her father in her youth as a result of her mother's early death. Her memories of her father are dominated by his tyranny and insensitivity. She cannot remember her father ever doing anything to make her believe that he loved her. She looks back to the day when she left home to go to college as a moment of liberation, when she was able to break free from his oppressive presence. The word *father* has, as a result, only negative associations. Ann has considerable personal difficulties about thinking of God as a "father," and has real doubts about whether God can be said to "love" her.

Bill has a track record of persistent failure, both in academic studies and personal relationships. His family places considerable emphasis upon success and the achievement of status, and have made it clear that they regard him as something of a disappointment. He hasn't met the standards of his high-achieving parents. As a result, he has now acquired a deeply ingrained sense of failure and personal inability. Bill finds the gospel intimidating, because it seems to make demands which he feels he cannot meet. He is frightened of failing God. He has genuine and deep doubts and anxieties about whether he can ever really be a Christian.

Clare has been through a series of broken personal relationships. She has experienced exploitation in relationships. And as a result she feels deeply hurt. She is also very reluctant to get involved in any further personal commitments as she fears the results. Her rather bitter experience of life has persuaded her that people cannot be trusted. Her experience of relationships leads her to believe that she only makes herself vulnerable and weak through trusting others, and allowing herself to become close to them. Consequently, she finds it difficult to commit herself to God. She feels he cannot be trusted. She is very reluctant to get involved in a relationship with him.

Many more examples could be given. But the basic idea is clear: your background can affect your faith. The situations you've been through in the past may cause you anxieties relating to your faith. Your past may predispose you to certain doubts, anxieties, and worries. In other words, present doubts may well reflect the continuing influence of past situations. Many people find it useful to try and identify the way in which their past affects their present, especially if this influence is unhelpful. You might like to try doing this with a sympathetic friend or counsellor.

However, the main point to be made here is simple: our doubts, anxieties and difficulties often reflect our individuality. You may see things in a different way from your friends, simply because you are who you are. You may worry about something that doesn't bother your best friend. You may find it difficult to understand why your best friend has problems where you have none. In part, this may just reflect the fact that you and your best friend are different people who have been through and been affected by different situations. Our doubts often mirror our situation and help us realize more about ourselves. If you want to help someone who has difficulties or anxieties about their faith, you may find you need to understand them as individuals before you can be much help. You may find that you can't give the same textbook answer to them all. So be sensitive to your own individuality and that of others. It may affect your faith and your doubts.

A further example will be helpful. Some people find it difficult to accept that God loves them. The reasons for their difficulties often reflect their background and the values instilled into them by their families. For example, they might be perfectionists who feel that they must *do* something or *achieve* something before God can love them. For this sort of person, the gospel proclamation of the *unconditionality* of God's love for us can be difficult to accept—it contradicts the standards of the world. Or they may have been taught that dependency is to be discouraged. Some individuals believe strongly in the cult of independence: personal fulfilment is based on not being dependent on anyone or anything. The idea

29

that God loves us is an invitation to learn to depend on God. This clashes with the set of values they have been taught by their families who are anxious that they should get ahead in the world through being independent. In both these cases, it is necessary to question how appropriate these values are, and whether they apply to our relationship with God. But the basic point remains the same: your past history can affect the way you react to the gospel and the difficulties you experience in relation to it.

Clare (mentioned above), also illustrates a point that is often overlooked. The word *doubt* can have two slightly different meanings. We could call these "cognitive" and "personal." The first doubts *statements*; the second doubts *persons*. One is a "doubt it," the other a "doubt you," problem. Let's begin by looking at a "doubt it" situation.

The New Testament provides us with an excellent illustration of this kind of doubt. After the resurrection Jesus appeared to his disciples. The disciples were both surprised and overjoyed (John 20:19–20). However, one of the disciples, Thomas, wasn't there on that occasion. He missed the experience the others had of the presence of the risen Christ. And, when they told him about it, he found it rather difficult to accept. He doubted it. "Unless I see the nail marks in his hands, and put my finger where the nails were, and put my hand into his side, I will not believe it" (John 20:25). Thomas doubted the belief of the other disciples that Jesus had been raised. That doubt was resolved through his encounter with the risen Christ, who spoke these words, "Stop doubting and believe" (John 20:27).

The second type of doubt is slightly different. Thomas

doubted *something*; you can also doubt *someone*. It's a "doubt you," not a "doubt it," situation. To doubt someone is to not trust them. It is to have difficulty in taking them at their word. Suppose I lent a colleague a large sum of money that he never repaid. He had promised to repay me. But it never happened. If he was to ask me to lend him some more money, I think I would hesitate before doing so! I would doubt his word. I would not have faith in his promises. I would not trust him. Clare illustrates the case where someone has profound difficulties in trusting God as a person. She is reluctant to commit herself because of her past experience of the untrustworthiness of people within relationships. She may not doubt that God exists; she does, however, doubt him as a person.

Clare is typical of many who have anxieties about whether God really can be trusted in the first place. Does he keep his promises? Does he really love us? That sort of doubt can cast so deep a shadow that everything else seems of little importance. Why worry about doubts or difficulties concerning Christian beliefs when God may not be worth believing in? Why bother about problems of Christian faith if you are hesitant about committing yourself to God in the first place? This is a "doubt you" problem. The gospel centers upon the absolute trustworthiness, goodness, and faithfulness of God as we know him and see him revealed in Jesus Christ. We shall therefore be dealing with some questions touching on the trustworthiness of God himself in the hope that this may help people with such anxieties.

There are obvious connections between doubt and faith. Each of them has this dual aspect. I can believe that certain things are true, just as I can doubt that they

31

are true. In part, this reflects the nature of the gospel itself. The gospel declares that certain things are *true*. For example, it insists that Jesus really did rise from the dead (1 Corinthians 15:3–5). It also makes some crucial affirmations about God himself. God is *trustworthy*; he is *faithful* (Romans 3:3; 1 Thessalonians 5:24). To doubt God is to question his faithfulness and reliability. We trust the *statement* that Jesus rose from the dead, but we trust the *person* of God. Of course, there is a close relation between these two ideas. One of the reasons why we can trust God is that he raised Jesus from the dead. It shows that he is faithful to his promises. It is, however, helpful to make this distinction between two aspects of "doubt" and "faith" at this early stage.

It is also important to appreciate that doubts concern more than God. Many Christians have doubts about themselves (perhaps reflecting their background and personal history), which spill over into their thinking about God. For this reason, I have tried to bring together in this book some of the more common doubts Christians have, and have grouped them together roughly into four categories: doubts about the gospel, about ourselves, about Jesus, and about God. Let's look at the idea of doubt more closely before going any further.

Biblical terms for doubt

The New Testament does not use one single word throughout to represent "doubt." Rather, it uses a range of words, each of which illuminates one particular aspect of what doubt really is. Each is like a snapshot of a landscape or a building: it's not good enough in itself to give a total picture, but it can give an excellent idea of what one aspect is like. And a series of snapshots builds up to give a total picture. There are four main images used in the New Testament, each of which illuminates one angle of the concept of doubt.

Hesitation. After his resurrection, Jesus appeared on a mountain to his disciples. Matthew describes the scene thus, "When they saw him, they worshiped him; but some doubted" (Matthew 28:17). Although all the disciples encountered the risen Christ, some clearly had difficulty in accepting what had happened. Perhaps they felt that it was too good to be true. Perhaps they were frightened and shocked by what happened. The word used here (Greek: *distazo*) has the sense of "to hold back" or "to hesitate." The same word and the same idea may be found earlier in Matthew's gospel (Matthew 14:31) in the description of the storm at sea. Here, Peter's lack of faith is shown in his hesitation to put his trust in Jesus. Hesitation betrays a lack of trust. If you hesitate to accept an offer, it's because you have misgivings about it. You may not trust the person who is making the offer. You may not understand what it implies. You suspect that there may be something wrong with it. Our reluctance to accept the gospel wholeheartedly, with the enthusiasm of little children, reflects a basic lack of trust in God and his promises. We hesitate to accept them. We hold back.

Indecision. In stressing the importance of faith to the individual believer, Jesus points out the need not to doubt (Matthew 21:21). Paul notes how Abraham trusted in God's promise, and "did not waver through unbelief" (Romans 4:20). The Greek word used here (*diakrino*) originally had the sense of "argue with," "to be at odds with," or "take issue with." This older meaning can still be seen in Acts 11:2, describing how Peter found himself in disputation with Jewish sympathizers in Jerusalem. However, in the New Testament, a developed meaning can be seen—to argue *with yourself*. The image is that of an internal mental debate reflecting indecision and a lack of conviction. The same idea and word is used in James 1:6, with a powerful image—a wave tossed by the wind in a stormy sea— which we shall explore further in a moment. You are divided within yourself, unsure of what to do.

In his letters, Paul frequently speaks of having "put off your old self" on becoming a Christian (Romans 6:6; Ephesians 4:22; Colossians 3:9). Part of the problem that many of us have is that our former unconverted self seems to live on! It is almost as if there is a debate going on between the "old self" and the "new self." The former is highly skeptical of God's promises, while the latter wants to embrace them wholeheartedly. The result? Indecision. Hesitation. Wavering. A lack of confidence in God. The very existence of doubt reminds us of how easy it is not to allow God into every part of our lives. We are reluctant to allow God to take control of us. It is as if we have opened the door of our life to the risen Christ (Revelation 3:20), but only allowed him a toehold in the house! We are reluctant to admit him fully. We treat him like a guest, when we ought to be treating him as the Lord. Doubt is thus a symptom of our lack of commitment to God.

Doubt is a way in which God is able to deepen our faith *by showing us our lack of faith*. The existence of doubt is like a signpost, showing us how far we have to go before we have fully committed ourselves to God. It shows up as sheer illusion any temptation we may have to rely upon ourselves rather than God. It is therefore with a sense of relief that we read Paul's words (Romans 3:3–4), reminding us that our lack of faith in no way alters God's faithfulness toward us! We can always turn to him in prayer, and ask him to help our unbelief. Like the man who came to Jesus, we can pray: "Lord, I believe! Help my unbelief!" (Mark 9:24).

Being of two minds. Doubters are described as "double-minded (*dipsychos*)" (James 4:8). To doubt is to be of two minds about something. It implies indecision, hesitation, and a resulting lack of progress. When I studied medieval philosophy at the university, I remember being intrigued by the problem known as "Buridan's Ass." (Actually, Buridan tells the story about a dog rather than an ass.) Suppose you have a hungry donkey placed midway between two piles of food. If it's going to survive, it will need to make a decision to eat one of them. But what happens if it can't make up its mind? In the end the unfortunate donkey dies, having been unable to make a decision about which pile of food to eat.

There's an obvious parallel here with doubt. We are confronted with two different options: to believe, or not to believe. It is very difficult to postpone a decision on this one. Each has its own very different rewards. Yet those rewards are only gained by commitment. For example, it would be very difficult for someone to adopt an "eat, drink, and be merry for tomorrow we die" attitude to life if he halfway believes in the resurrection and future divine judgment. Likewise, it would be difficult for a Christian to take the great gospel promises of resurrection and eternal life seriously if he halfway believes that there is nothing after death. Each of these individuals is of two minds; they have a foot in each camp. People like that are in the same position as Buridan's ass—they can't benefit from either pile of food.

Doubt means not having resolved an inner conflict between unbelief and faith. It means keeping options open long after we ought to have closed them. Jesus told his disciples that they were to be *in* the world but not *of* the world (John 17:6–16). They live in the world, but their hope lies beyond it. They do not conform to its standards and its unbelief. *There will always be a tension between the believer and the world.* In part, doubt arises through having feet in the camps of both the world and the gospel and being reluctant to make that break. For many people there is security in staying within something that is known (however unsatisfactory) just as there is unease about confronting the unknown. "Play it safe!" is the motto of many. Some are reluctant to commit themselves to the gospel because it seems otherworldly. But the New Testament sees commitment to the gospel as the essential starting point for developing a right attitude to the world. No longer need we be frightened by death; no longer are we hypnotized by wealth (Matthew 6:19–21). We are enabled to live *in* the world without giving in to its standards and its anxieties.

Doubt as a state of mind. Thomas found it difficult to believe that Jesus had risen from the dead. Jesus, knowing this, spoke these words to him: "Stop doubting and believe" (John 20:27). The Greek phrase used is quite difficult to translate into English. Greek has two forms of imperative. In other words, you can tell somebody to do something in two different ways. What is known as an *aorist imperative* means, "Do this action once." If I asked somebody to open a window, I would use this form. A second form, however, is the *present imperative*. This means, "Keep on doing this! Don't just do it once!" The Greek verb used in John 20:27 is a present imperative. It doesn't mean, "On this one occasion, don't doubt—believe instead"! Rather, it means, "Stop doubting now, once and for all. And keep on believing." In other words, doubt and faith are both states of mind or attitudes. Doubt is a constant attitude of *questioning* toward God, where faith is a constant attitude of *trust and openness*. We are being asked to develop a permanent attitude of openness and trust toward God—not just to be open to him and trust him on any one occasion, but to be like this all the time. And, as we saw above, this results in conflict at times because our old tendency to doubt God surfaces, underscoring our need to commit ourselves more fully to him.

Biblical images of doubt

Two images are particularly helpful in thinking about the nature and effects of doubt, and beginning to develop ways of handling it.

Walking in the dark

"Our salvation is nearer now than when we first believed. The night is nearly over; the day is almost here" (Romans 13:11–12). These phrases from Paul invite us to think of the Christian life as walking in the dark. The dawn is now nearer than when we first began that walk; but it has yet to happen. In the meantime, we have to cross an unknown landscape hoping that we will arrive safely at our destination. We cannot fully see the road ahead of us; nevertheless, we trust in the Lord to guide us home. "We live by faith, not by sight" (2 Corinthians 5:7).

Imagine you are a traveler in medieval England. You decide to travel to Oxford from the nearby village of Witney. Darkness falls as you near Oxford so that you cannot see the landscape around you. You decide to keep going along the road despite the darkness. All you can see is the road ahead of you, which you know to have been signposted to Oxford. At times there are things about that road that puzzle you. The road may turn abruptly to the left at one point. Why, you wonder. At another point, it becomes very muddy. Again, you wonder why. But you don't know. You can't see the full picture. You're in the dark.

Of course, when dawn breaks you see the landscape fully illuminated. Then the real state of things becomes apparent. You might suddenly notice that the road swerves to the left to avoid an open mineshaft, invisible to you in the dark. You might see that at one point the road passes close to a raging torrent, which might have swept you away if the road had not led you away from it—as it turned out, all that happened was that your feet got muddy. Although you could not understand what was happening at the time, you subsequently realize that the road led you in safety in the darkness through a series of dangers. Your initial bewilderment turns to relief. The same point is made by the English writer P. G. Wodehouse in relating how Bertie Wooster was saved by his faithful manservant Jeeves from a potentially disastrous marriage to Honoria Glossop (daughter of a distinguished psychiatrist, who is convinced that Wooster is mentally deficient). Jeeves behaves in a way that Wooster cannot understand, leading him to doubt his faithfulness. Then the moment of insight dawns.

I realized all in a flash how I had been wronging this faithful fellow. All the while I supposed he had been landing me in the soup, he had really been steering me away from it. It was like those stories one used to read as a kid about the traveller going along on a dark night and his dog grabs him by the leg of his trousers and he says "Down, sir! What are you doing, Rover?" and the dog hangs on and he gets rather hot under the collar and curses a bit but the dog won't let him go and then suddenly the moon shines through the clouds and he finds he's been standing on the edge of a precipice and one more step would have—well, anyway, you get the idea.

The basic point here is that we don't see the full picture. God does; we don't. As Paul puts it, we "see but a poor reflection as in a mirror" (1 Corinthians 13:12). It's like being inside a car on a dark night, with the windows fogged up. You can't see properly. There are many things about the Christian life that puzzle us. Yet we have to learn to live with the fact that we will never see the full picture, and for that very reason, we will have to put up with areas of experience that seem contradictory and confusing. Doubt arises partly because we feel frustrated at not being able to understand everything. We want to stand in the place of God, and be able to survey the landscape across which the path of faith must travel. Yet we can't. In fact, we can't really see further than the end of our spiritual noses! We believe passionately and rightly that there is a road there, that it will lead us safely to our goal, and that Jesus Christ has been along that road before us like a pioneer or trailblazer (Hebrews 12:1–3). But we don't understand exactly what is going on at points. Our place

39

is *on* that path, not *above* it. One day, we firmly believe, all will be made clear—but this will be on the far side of our resurrection! For the moment, however, we must walk through the darkness in faith and hope.

However, the landscape is not totally dark. The image of light is used frequently by scriptural writers reminding us that God has not left us completely in the dark! Scripture itself guides us as we walk. "Your word is a lamp to my feet and a light for my path" (Psalm 119:105). This helpful image suggests illumination of an area around us while we walk, but not of the entire landscape. Again, it's like being in a car at night, with the headlights illuminating a small area just ahead of us. The important thing is that we find our way home, not that we understand exactly what is happening at every point along the way! The road really is there, tried and tested by previous generations of travellers. John Henry Newman gave powerful expression to the idea of Jesus Christ as the light of the world, guiding sinners home to safety, in his poem *Lead, Kindly Light.*

> Lead, kindly light, amid the encircling gloom;
>> Lead thou me on;
>> The night is dark, and I am far from home;
>> Lead thou me on.
> Keep thou my feet; I do not ask to see
>> The distant scene; one step enough for me.

The famous gospel image of a city on a hill (Matthew 5:14–16) makes the same point: a light shining in the darkness can guide us home. Take one step at a time, and don't be frightened by the thought of how long or difficult that journey might be. God will be with you, traveling alongside you and lighting your path as he accompanies you on your way.

So it is understandable that doubt should arise on account of our less than total grasp of the situation. We aren't fully in the picture. But how important is this? Isn't what really matters the fact that God promises to be faithful to us, to remain with us as we travel, to guide us and support us? And that Christ has gone before us to prepare a place for us? The gospel doesn't pretend to explain every aspect of our life as believers—it does, however, promise that God will be with us throughout that life (Psalm 23). In the end, it is the saving presence of God in the life of believers that matters more than a complete explanation of the way things are. Anyway, how could we finite creatures ever hope to gain a total understanding of our situation?

A rough sea

"He who doubts is like a wave of the sea, blown and tossed by the wind" (James 1:6). This is a very powerful image, especially for anyone who has ever been violently seasick! The image evoked by James is of lack of stability. The sea—along with anything that happens to be floating in it—is tossed to and fro by the wind, unable to gain stability. Seasickness is basically caused by a disruption of the human sense of balance arising from this instability. You lose your bearings. Life is miserable, and you long for the ship to regain its stability. Doubt in the Christian life is rather like permanent seasickness on a long ocean voyage. So how can stability be regained?

God's faithfulness is like an anchor (Hebrews 6:18–19). He is true to his promises, giving us something that we can hold on to. Just as a ship being blown off course by a storm might lower its anchor, so faith in God gives us direction and stability in life. It's like a lifeline thrown to us in a raging sea: in the midst of this storm, we can find peace in the trustworthy promises of God. It offers us stability and safety. The death of Jesus Christ on the cross of Calvary demonstrates both God's overwhelming love for us and his commitment to us. Nothing can cancel his faithfulness to us. Like a harbor, he offers refuge from the storms of life. Doubt means having nothing to hold on to in this situation. It means a lack of trust in the means of security God is offering us. Faith, on the other hand, means trusting the faithfulness of God and the reliability of the assistance which he offers us (Psalm 119:35–40).

Who is this book for?

There are two types of situations in which you might pick up this book. It may be you, yourself, who is worried by doubt. You may be very hesitant to admit it, but in your heart of hearts you know that you hope to be helped by this book yourself. Please read the first section that follows below before going any further. It may be helpful.

On the other hand, it may be that a friend of yours is worried about something, and you hope to be able to help. The second section below is for you if this is the case. In the final chapter, we'll return to look at some further ways of handling doubt. But some introductory comments at this stage are in order.

It's my problem

Many Christians find themselves feeling very guilty about doubt. They feel that they have somehow let God down. Sometimes they even try to hide the fact from

God. This may be your case. As a result you may feel that God is far away, and that he is not worth praying to. You may even feel tempted to give up being a Christian. If this is the case, you can take some comfort from the fact that thoughts very much like this are expressed in Scripture. Moses, Jeremiah, and David are all examples of great biblical people of faith who wrestled with doubt. It's not just you fighting against doubt all on your own. Countless men and women down through the ages have faced the same struggle.

Read Psalm 42 carefully and slowly. Notice how honest the psalmist is. He tells God how he feels. He remembers the times when he felt close to God (v. 4). He thinks that God has forgotten him (v. 9). His friends are making fun of him because of his doubts (v. 10). He feels far away from God. Perhaps you find your own thoughts echoed as you read the Psalm. Take comfort from the fact that you're not the first to feel this way! You're in excellent company. But notice also how he brings all these things to God in prayer. He doesn't try to keep them from God. It is by keeping up his time of prayer that his experience of God will be restored and renewed. Notice how the Psalm ends with a marvellous statement of hope (v. 11): he will praise God again. Make that hope yours.

Read Psalm 139:1–12. Notice the constant theme: God knows us. Our thoughts are no secret to him. So be honest in your prayers: tell God how you feel, and how difficult it is for you. You may feel far away from God, but see how the psalmist affirms that, no matter how far he goes away, God is still with him (vv. 8–12). Just as a cloud passes before the sun, and obscures its light, so something may have come between you and God. *But he is still there, irrespective of your feelings.* Now look at the final two verses (23–24). The psalmist tells God of his "anxious thoughts," and asks God to search his heart and test him—in other words, to help him identify what the matter might be. Like Psalm 42, the ending is positive, reflecting the sure confidence in the faithfulness of the Lord, so powerful a theme of Old and New Testaments alike, and so constant a feature of Christian experience down through the ages (Hebrews 10:23).

The fact that the faithfulness of God is not contradicted by a sense of his absence is brought out in a short piece, "Footprints in the Sand."

> One night I had a dream. I dreamed I was walking along the beach with God, and across the sky flashed scenes from my life. For each scene I noticed two sets of footprints in the sand; one belonged to me and the other to God. When the last scene of my life flashed before us I looked back at the footprints in the sand. I noticed that at times along the path of life there was only one set of footprints.
>
> I also noticed that it happened at the very lowest and saddest times of my life. This really bothered me and I questioned God about it. "God, you said that once I decided to follow you, you would walk with me all the way, but I noticed that during the most troublesome times in my life there is only one set of footprints. I don't understand why in times when I needed you most, you would leave me." God replied, "My precious, precious child, I love you and I would never, never leave you during your times of trials and suffering. When you see only one set of footprints, it was then that I carried you."

Don't stop going to church or keeping company with other Christians if you feel you're going through a dry spell. Their support can keep you going. God may speak to you through a sermon or a scriptural passage to reassure you of his love for you. Your faith may be

44

brought back to life through the words of a hymn or song, or through a sense of the presence of God. Don't make it difficult for God to comfort and reassure you. Give him the opportunities. That's why it's important to try to keep some sort of regular pattern of prayer.

Try also to think about what you are doing when you pray. Many people allow prayer to become something mechanical, a routine series of requests. This idea of prayer is seriously deficient. Discover the *richness* of prayer. Read some works that will show you how rich and satisfying prayer can be (see "For further reading").

The Psalms often speak about "waiting patiently for the Lord" (Psalm 27:14; 33:20; 130:5–6). Read these passages: can you see how the psalmist is aware of God's absence at that moment, yet is confident that the Lord, who is faithful to his promises, will come to those who put their trust in him? The reason that those Psalms are there in the Old Testament is to comfort and reassure those who feel the same way today. Their confidence in God's faithfulness can be yours as well.

It's someone else's problem

Try to be gentle, sensitive and caring. "Be merciful to those who doubt" (Jude 22). It's very easy to give your friend the impression that your main interest is his or her scalp! If you lack sensitivity, your friend may think you're acting like the Spanish Inquisition. There's a world of difference between demanding that your friend toe the line on every point of faith and a genuine concern for his or her well-being and spiritual development. Your desire to help your friend must reflect a genuine love for him or her as a person, as well as a love of God and conviction that the gospel is of urgent

45

importance. Counseling must be person-centered as well as issue-centered. As I will emphasize in the final chapter of this book, doubt can arise through personal difficulties. Anxieties about money, work, family, or personal relationships can spill over into the life of faith. Remember how Jesus talked about "the worries of this life, the deceitfulness of wealth and the desires for other things" (Mark 4:19) that stopped the Word of God from growing properly. Your friend may talk about doubting God, but it is quite possible that the real problem is located elsewhere. Try to explore this, possibly along the lines suggested in the final chapter.

Try to keep in mind how fragile and vulnerable a thing faith is, especially if your friend has come to faith recently. The New Testament uses a whole range of images to get this idea across. And it's not just those who have become Christians recently who need to grow in faith. Remember how Jesus even called the disciples "you of little faith" (Matthew 8:26; 14:31), and how the apostles asked him to increase their faith (Luke 17:5). So what is faith like?

It's like a plant (Mark 4:30–32). It starts off as a tiny seed and grows up. But when it's still young it is tender and vulnerable. When a gardener plants seeds in a patch of ground he'll fence off the area to stop people from walking on it so they won't damage the young seedlings. Later on, the plants can cope with this, but in their first stages of growth they need to be protected. Maybe you've seen an area of ground in your local park or campus that's been sown recently with grass seed: eventually, you can walk all over it, but to start with it has to be protected so that it can grow. It's just like that with faith.

46

Difficulties of some kind or other are fairly natural in the first stages of the Christian life. They are like some sort of spiritual growing pains. You often hear it said that faith is "caught, not taught." As they grow in experience, you may find that younger Christians will outgrow some of their initial problems. But faith is not just trust in God—it is belief in certain quite definite things about God, about Jesus, and about ourselves. And as the young Christian begins to explore what his or her faith means it is quite likely that he or she will come up against difficulties at points. The eleventh-century writer Anselm of Canterbury spoke of "faith seeking understanding." By this he meant that an individual comes to faith and then has to start working through what that faith involves. Trust in God comes first; understanding the Christian faith comes second. And you ought to be able to help young Christians with some of the difficulties they encounter while trying to *understand* their faith, perhaps along the lines suggested in the next four chapters.

But this isn't really doubt. It's more a kind of learning process in which older Christians can play a very helpful and positive role. You may be able to remember some of the difficulties you had when you first became a Christian and be able to draw on that experience to help your friend. The New Testament always treats faith as something dynamic rather than static—it's something which *develops*. The young Christian may not be doubting something—he or she may just not be ready for it at this stage. The New Testament uses a very helpful analogy to bring out this point (1 Corinthians 3:2; Hebrews 5:12; 1 Peter 2:2). Babies are unable to digest solid food to start with, and so drink milk. At some point, they can be transferred from milk to solid food. They can be weaned. So, if a young Christian has problems with some aspect of the Christian faith, don't assume that they are plagued by doubt! They may just not be ready for that aspect of the faith. It may be indigestible at this stage. The idea that they find difficult may be like the piece of solid food a baby cannot digest. There's nothing wrong with either the food or the child: it's just that the child hasn't yet reached the stage when it can cope with that sort of food.

So be especially sensitive to the needs of young Christians. Like seeds, they are growing, and need shelter and support. Like young babies, they are not yet ready for the staple diet of adults. What you may see as doubt may well be part of the process of growing and developing. You can help. You can explain things to them, you can share your experiences of growing up as a Christian, and you can point them in the direction of useful books that they might find helpful. Just as Paul spoke of watering the ground in which seeds are growing (1 Corinthians 3:6–8), you can help stop the ground from drying up. You can remember them in your prayers and offer to be of practical assistance. As the parable of the sower makes clear, it's very often external pressures which cause problems for faith (Mark 4:18–19). By helping to relieve those pressures, you can help your friend to deepen his or her faith. We'll explore this further in the final chapter. And don't hesitate to suggest that your friend spend time with some older Christian whom you trust—perhaps a local minister or pastor.

A further difficulty can arise through unrealistic expectations. Young Christians can easily substitute their own expectations of what God ought to do in place of what God wants to do. For example, they may expect God to convert their unbelieving parents during the next school break. This can easily lead to doubt when God does not do what they feel he ought to, or what they expect or want him to do. It is important to explain the need to wait patiently and trust in God's timetable, rather than impose our own upon him (2 Peter 3:8).

But some of your friends may have real doubts about certain specific matters. Hopefully this book will give you some ideas about how you can help them with these doubts. We begin by exploring a series of doubts people have about the gospel itself.

Questions for discussion
- How would you distinguish these three different ideas: doubt, lack of certainty, unbelief?
- In what ways can doubt paralyze your faith?
- What are the most common doubts people have about Christianity?
- Are there any factors in your own background that make you prone to some special doubt?

Doubts about the Gospel

Chapter 2

Doubts about the Gospel

We begin by considering two anxieties about the gospel itself. First, some young Christians, especially students, often have a secret uneasiness about the future of Christianity. Will it go out of date? Are they committing themselves to something that may become an irrelevance in their old age? A second anxiety concerns the effectiveness of the gospel. Some Christians become despondent because of the apparent ineffectiveness of their attempts to proclaim the gospel, and sometimes wonder if this reflects some fundamental weakness, perhaps even a fatal flaw, in the gospel itself. We shall address these anxieties in what follows.

Will Christianity go out of fashion sometime?

We live in times when everything seems to become obsolete very quickly. The latest technology makes current methods and equipment go out of date with alarming speed. And it isn't just hardware that gets outdated in this way. Ideas go out of fashion very quickly. I grew up in the 1960s, when it seemed to many that the Western world was going through a period of revolution. Commonly held ideas and standards were being thrown out as irrelevant. We were told that the world had come of age, and that it no longer needed the "outdated" ideas of past generations. There was much talk of the "death of God" on the university campuses of North America and elsewhere. Christianity was portrayed as outmoded and irrelevant to the needs of this brave new world.

Of course, the 1960s were a long time ago. Looking back, it is the ideas of the 1960s which have become outdated. They've gone out of fashion. Instead of being a permanent feature of the way we think, they were shown up to be a response to the needs of that period. As time passed and the situation changed they lost their credibility. They had a shelf life of about a decade before they became unmarketable. Christianity has been a powerful force in the world for nearly two thousand years and shows no sign of losing its appeal. Marxism argued that, when the revolution came, Christianity would be abandoned as outdated and pointless; in fact, the reverse occurred with a new interest in the Christian faith developing within Marxist states, despite government programs designed to eliminate it. In America in the 1960s it was suggested that there was an urgent need to find an alternative religion on account of the new outlook on life which was allegedly developing in Western civilization. But, as history has shown, it was that new outlook on life, rather than Christianity, that was found to be irrelevant to the needs and aspirations of human beings.

But this does raise an important question. Is Christianity itself something that will go out of fashion in the future? As time passes and the human situation changes, will the gospel cease to be relevant? After all, nobody believes in the old Roman or Greek gods any more—yet they seem to have been influential for a while. This is a cause of special concern to college and university students: is the Christian gospel in which they have placed their trust (or in which they are thinking of placing their trust) something to which they can hold fast for the remainder of their lives? Or will it cease to have any relevance after a decade? Doubts of this kind trouble a number of young Christians, and may cause others to hesitate before committing themselves. It is therefore important to deal with this question fully.

Two answers may be given to this doubt. First, the gospel addresses a fundamental problem of human nature, which progress hasn't altered. Second, if it really is *God* who is behind the gospel, it cannot lose its power and appeal. We'll look at these individually.

The human dilemma remains the same

The gospel is not some form of human wisdom that will be outdated within a matter of years, but an eternally relevant message concerning God and ourselves, and especially the relationship established through the death and resurrection of Jesus Christ. The human dilemma remains the same yesterday, today, and forever—the need to be loved, the need to have hope in the face of death, the need to break free from sin. The gospel identifies these deep longings and needs within human nature.

The gospel does not, however, merely diagnose the human situation: it offers to transform it. It doesn't just identify our problems, but proclaims their solution. It affirms the overwhelming love of God for sinners, and draws our attention to the astonishing extent to which God will go to demonstrate that love. It offers to break the stranglehold of human sin, setting us free to live with God. It offers us a firm and unshakable hope in the face of death. And so long as human beings walk the face of this earth, knowing that they must die, the gospel of the resurrection of Jesus Christ will continue to address a basic human need. Let's develop this point a little.

In his recent book *The Denial of Death*, Ernest Becker points out how much human activity is based on an illusion. Unlike other animals, humans know that they are going to die, and cannot cope with the thought. They spend much of their time trying to deny the inevitability of death, creating the illusion that death is always something which happens to somebody else. Death is something that people prefer not to talk about because of the anxiety it causes. And so life becomes a desperate denial of human mortality. This denial is merely a crutch on which many are totally dependent for their sanity. Death, as someone once grimly remarked, is the ultimate statistic.

But how can anyone base their entire life on a total delusion? Running away from reality won't change the situation. It is perfectly understandable that people should be afraid of death. But that is precisely why the gospel is so important and so relevant! Through his death and resurrection, Jesus Christ is able to "free those who all their lives were held in slavery by their fear of death" (Hebrews 2:15). This power to liberate individuals from the fear of death is not some after-thought—it is central to the gospel theme.

The gospel is the work of God, not a human invention

When Paul preached the gospel at Corinth, he was acutely aware of his own deficiencies as a preacher. Yet, despite this, the gospel took root there. He later wrote to the church at Corinth concerning his poor performance (1 Corinthians 2:1–5),

> When I came to you, brothers, I did not come with eloquence or superior wisdom as I proclaimed to you the testimony about God. For I resolved to know nothing while I was with you except Jesus Christ and him crucified. I came to you in weakness and fear, and with much trembling. My message and my preaching were not with wise and persuasive words, but with a demonstration of the Spirit's power, so that your faith might not rest on men's wisdom, but on God's power.

Can you see what Paul is saying here? The gospel that he proclaimed, and that won the hearts and minds of the Corinthian Christians, is not a human invention but is the work of God.

Much the same point is made elsewhere in the New Testament. "We did not follow cleverly invented stories when we told you about the power and coming of our Lord Jesus Christ, but we were eyewitnesses of his majesty" (2 Peter 1:16). In other words, the gospel isn't based on human wisdom or invention, but upon the revelation of God in history, seen and attested by eyewitnesses. The death and resurrection of Jesus were no fiction or legend—they were events in history seen and proclaimed by the first Christians (1 Corinthians 15:3–8).

If you accept the gospel, you may rest assured that you are not committing intellectual suicide by falling victim to some fleeting whim which will have passed into the footnotes of history books within a few years. The gospel is not like some cult, craze, or fashion, that is abandoned when something else takes its place. And why not? Because we are not dealing with some human invention, some ideas that somebody thought up, but rather with the gracious self-revelation of God himself, a revelation that both declares and meets the spiritual needs of humanity. Whoever you are and wherever you live, the gospel has the power to convert you, and, having converted you, to hold you. It is God's gospel, the gospel that he revealed and for which his Son died upon the cross of Calvary.

If God really is behind the gospel, it cannot fail. In his wisdom and his love God has given to us the good news of forgiveness through the death of Jesus Christ. If God cannot judge what is going to be relevant to us, who can? Your faith rests not in human wisdom (which is likely to be rejected by later generations), but in the power of God—the same God who was able to raise Jesus Christ from the dead, thus transforming a scene of hopelessness and helplessness to one of joy and triumph. This is the kind of God who inspires confidence. Your friends may think you foolish for your faith, as others thought Paul foolish before you—but you may rest assured, as Paul did before you, that the gospel which has touched your heart today is not from human beings but from God, and it will continue to proclaim the saving love of God in Christ until he comes again.

The gospel seems to have little effect on my friends

Let's begin by putting this in perspective. It's a big decision you're asking your friends to make. You're asking them to commit themselves to God. You're asking them to dedicate their lives to Jesus Christ. Now that's a lot to ask of anyone! So you must expect a certain degree of hesitation on their part. They will want to weigh the consequences. They will want to think the matter through. They won't want to rush into it. That's reasonable.

In fact, it's such a big decision that many people prefer to take it in small stages. Think of each individual having his or her own personal road to faith. Everyone has different needs and problems. The result is that it's difficult to lay down in advance what a "typical" conversion might be like. For some, that road may be relatively short and easy. But for others, it may be long and difficult. Think of yourself as helping them a little further along that road or helping them around obstacles which are strewn in their path. You may not help them all the way to the final destination, but you can leave them nearer than when they started. They may end up by feeling much more positive toward Christianity and toward Christians on account of you. Perhaps they may find they have fewer difficulties with some of its ideas as a result of talking to you. Maybe you plant some seeds that will germinate later. However, it's quite likely that they won't admit this and you won't realize what's happening. And so you get discouraged.

Jesus told a parable that is helpful and relevant here. Mark 4:26–29 relates how someone scatters seed on the ground, and then leaves it. The seed grows in secret, eventually to break through the ground and mature. Most commentators on this passage see it as referring to the hidden working of the kingdom of God in the world. Its effects are not initially seen; it is growing in secret, like the seed beneath the ground. It can't be seen—but that doesn't mean it's not there. The parable makes clear the importance of sowing the seed (see also Ecclesiastes 11:6). That's our responsibility. But it is God who makes the seed grow (cf. 1 Corinthians 3:6–7), even if that process of growth can't be seen until the seedling bursts through the soil.

One of my favorite books is *The Diary of a Nobody*. It's a fictional diary recording the problems and aspirations of a lower-middle-class man (Mr. Pooter) and his family in late Victorian London. At one point, the diary tells of how Mr. Pooter sowed some seeds in his garden one evening. The entries for the next few days all record his growing desperation. Each day, he inspects his seeds—nothing has happened! There is something of Mr. Pooter in all of us: we want to see instant results from our witness to our friends. Conversion is something that must happen in the short term! But for many, conversion is a prolonged experience. *Your* only contribution may be to move them further down the road to faith.

Have you noticed how often Jesus returns to the theme of the goodness of the seed? The parable of the sower (Mark 4:3–8) stresses that it is the same good seed that falls into different kinds of ground. There's nothing wrong with the seed—it's the ground that makes the difference. What is important is that you scatter the seed. You cannot be sure what sort of ground it will fall upon. Some seed may be sown to no effect (perhaps being eaten by birds)—but that does *not* mean that the next seed you sow will fail to grow! Again, the seed may not seem to be growing (Mark 4:26–29) but, as Mr. Pooter eventually found out, that doesn't mean that there's anything wrong with it. It's important to have confidence in the power of the gospel, and trust that God will do his best with the seed that takes root through our witness. If the seed was no good, Christianity would have ceased to exist long ago.

It's helpful to think of Paul here. Try and imagine how the early church felt about Saul of Tarsus. Saul was, by all accounts, one of the most efficient persecutors of Christianity (Acts 8:1; 9:1–2). In a later letter, he recalled how intensely he persecuted the church, and how he tried to wipe it off the face of the earth (Galatians 1:13). Those first Christians could have been forgiven for thinking that Saul was an impossible case. Here, surely, was a nut that was too hard to crack. The gospel was having no visible effect on him. They must have been very discouraged.

The remarkable story of Paul's conversion through his encounter with the risen Christ (Acts 9:1–19; 22:2–16; 26:12–23) reminds us of two things. First, that it is *God* who is at work in the process of conversion. It isn't as if someone is converted on account of our eloquence, wisdom or arguments. Rather, it is God who is secretly at work in the hearts of men and women. In the end, conversion is about a transforming and redeeming encounter between an individual and the living Lord. We can help bring that about—but the encounter is God's doing, not ours. Second, it reminds us that the most unpromising outward appearances may conceal hidden signs of the work of God. Don't be anxious—

61

trust instead in the gospel, and the God who stands behind it.

In dealing with these two anxieties, you may find it helpful to read the story of the locked room (John 20:19–31). From that room, a very small group of people went out to convert the world—a seemingly impossible mission. Yet your faith can be traced back to that locked room. You have a spiritual family tree that connects you with someone who was there in that locked room on that momentous occasion. Through the faithfulness of that person, and those who followed him or her, you came to faith. That remarkable fact points to the power of the gospel to reach down the ages, across both centuries and continents. That ought to reassure you of its relevance and vitality! But it ought also to challenge you to ask a very important question. The great chain of events that leads from the locked room to you—where will it go next? To whom will *you* pass on the gospel proclamation? Or will you be a weak link in this chain? This sobering thought neatly brings us on to the next group of anxieties experienced by many, centering on their adequacy as Christians.

Questions for discussion

- How many religious movements can you think of that developed recently, and are now generally regarded as irrelevant?
- In what ways can you discern the influence of God upon your own journey to faith?
- Why do many people think that the gospel is foolish?
- How do parables about seeds help us understand the way the gospel is at work in the world?

Doubts about yourself

Chapter 3

Doubts about yourself

A second group of anxieties centers on our own relationship with God and especially our adequacy as Christians. Some Christians find it difficult to have any confidence in themselves. As a result, they find it hard to enter into Christian life in all its fullness with both its privileges and responsibilities. Unease over whether you really are a Christian, uncertainty over your abilities, or anxiety concerning your inadequacies—all these can induce a kind of mental and spiritual paralysis preventing you from developing and growing in faith and obedience. I hope that the present chapter will alleviate some of these anxieties.

I'm not sure that I am a Christian

This doubt is often experienced by people who have become Christians recently. How, they may ask, can they *know* that they are Christians? Is there something they can point to that proves that they really have been accepted by God? Is there some visible sign that proves they have entered into the kingdom of God? The early stage of faith is often a very vulnerable period, and it is not uncommon for Christians in their first stage of development to feel anxious about their relationship with God.

Don't rely on your feelings. In the following section, we will explore further how your feelings can sometimes be unreliable as a guide to your standing with God. Your feelings are tied up with many things. You may feel far from God on account of anxiety over your career, your work, a personal relationship, or financial difficulties. All of these can easily spill over into your perception of your relationship with God.

Instead, rely on the promises of God. These are outside of you, independent of your feelings and anxieties. Your feelings are subjective. God's promises are objective—they don't depend on your feelings. For example, look at God's promise to Joshua (Joshua 1:9). God promises to be with Joshua wherever he goes. He doesn't promise to be with Joshua on condition that Joshua *feels* that he is present! The promise of the presence of God is unconditional. Learn to mistrust your normal feelings at this point. "Be still, and know that I am God" (Psalm 46:10). We ought to ground our faith in the promises of God, recorded in Scripture and confirmed in Jesus Christ—not in the way we feel!

In one sense, these promises are *conditional*: they depend upon you having repented of your sins and having turned to God in faith. Faith is saying "Yes!" to God, learning to trust in him—to know him better—and to be obedient to him. Are you doing that? Remember that the Greek word usually translated as "repent" has the basic meaning of "turn around." You must turn around to face God (how many people spend their lives running away from God?), admit your sins and accept God's offer of forgiveness and eternal life. That can be painful and difficult for it involves admitting a need for God. Think of God offering you a gift. To receive it, you must stretch out your hand and receive it. The offer is real, as is the gift; your acceptance of the offer must be real as well. And if you have acccpted that offer, then you *are* a Christian. The promises of God are yours.

What sort of promises might these be? We shall look at three key promises. First, there is the promise that God, while detesting sin, loves sinners. "God demonstrates his own love for us in this: While we were still sinners, Christ died for us" (Romans 5:8). The full extent of this love is revealed in the cross of Christ. Jesus died in order to convince and assure us of the tender love of God for sinners (John 3:16), and thus to bring us home to God. Some people feel that they are too deeply immersed in their sin to be loved by God; the New Testament happens to take a very different view, affirming that *nothing* can separate us from the love of God in Christ (Romans 8:31–39). God's purpose and power to defeat sin are revealed in the cross. To suggest or imagine that *your* sin is somehow worse than anyone else's is to deny God the opportunity to break sin's power in your life. Try to imagine the situation Paul found himself in. How could God love him when he had persecuted the church of God? If anyone ever felt convinced of sin and personal inadequacy, that person was Paul. Yet Paul was able to draw on the tender mercy of God toward sinners and to speak of the remarkable effects of God's grace in his life (1 Corinthians 15:9–10).

67

There is a story told about the Scottish pastor and writer John Duncan that is relevant here. Duncan was conducting a service of Holy Communion in a local Church of Scotland parish. When he came to administer the wine to the congregation, a sixteen-year-old girl refused to accept it. She motioned with her hand, indicating that she did not feel able to share in the cup. Realizing that the girl felt unworthy to receive it, Duncan reached out, laid his arm on her shoulder, and said, "Take it lassie. It's meant for us sinners." The wine is a symbol of God's forgiveness of sins through the death of Christ—*real* forgiveness of *real* sins. To recognize the full extent of your sinfulness is not to disqualify yourself from the grace of God—it is to indicate how much you need it.

In the second place, we are promised forgiveness of sins (1 John 1:9). To become a Christian is to set the past behind us and to go forward into eternal life in the presence of the God who loved us and gave his only son for us. Through the cross, the burden of our sin is taken from us by Christ and his righteousness becomes ours (2 Corinthians 5:21). This promise of forgiveness, however, does not merely concern the *beginning* of your life as a Christian. You don't stop sinning when you become a Christian! Rather, you begin a long and hard struggle against sin. It can be very difficult at times. You will often feel that you have let God down. But learn to trust in God's immense kindness and tenderness: ask his forgiveness of these sins and start out all over again. Being a Christian isn't easy, as the New Testament stresses. All of us find it difficult going at times, which is why the news that God forgives us for our shortcomings and weaknesses is such good news.

In the third place, we are promised that God will stand by us in our lives as Christians. He will never leave us or forsake us (John 10:28). He is with us always (Matthew 28:20). No matter how we may feel God has promised to remain with us. He is the shepherd who guides us and guards us; who journeys with us, consoling us with his presence (Psalm 23). There is no small print qualifying this promise! God promises himself to all those who turn to him in faith.

Have you turned to God in faith and repentance? If you have, these promises concern you. You may feel that your faith is very weak. But, as we have stressed throughout this book, faith is like a plant—it is something that grows. The weakness and fragility of its early stages give way to the strength and maturity of its later phases. Some seeds germinate more rapidly than others, just as some plants grow more quickly than others. Be patient! Remember that a house that is built quickly is usually a house that is built badly—it won't survive! After all, even Rome wasn't built in a day. This slow and gradual growth in faith reflects human weakness and fragility, not any inability on God's part. God knows what we are like and how best to handle us. As Paul stresses (1 Corinthians 3:10–13), the Christian life is built securely upon a reliable foundation. If the seed of faith is firmly planted, it will grow—despite its initial fragility and vulnerability. The important thing is not that your faith is strong, but that you have faith! Like Paul, you can be "confident of this, that he who began a good work in you will carry it on to completion" (Philippians 1:6; cf. 2 Peter 1:3–4).

Be assured that God has done everything necessary for your salvation, and has done it well. Your salvation does not depend upon your personal merit, or your activity. God offers you his salvation—*real* salvation—as a gift. You are being asked to receive it, to accept it and make it your own. Julian of Norwich, a medieval English nun, wrote a fascinating book entitled *Revelations of Divine Love*, in which she stated, "the one thing that matters is that we always say Yes to God when we experience him." Say "Yes!" and all that God is and all that he means can be yours. Two illustrations may prove helpful. Imagine that you are in a darkened room. Outside, the sunlight is beaming down. However, there is a shutter in front of the window preventing the light from entering. You can open that shutter. By doing so, you are removing the only remaining obstacle to the light of the sun, thus allowing the sun to illuminate the room. You are not being asked to undertake the mammoth task of generating the heat and light of the sun—that has all been taken care of for you. Your sole task—but a task that *only* you can do—is to remove an obstacle to its passage. It is a relatively small task, but an essential one. If you have anxieties about whether you really are a Christian, ask yourself whether there are any remaining obstacles to God. Are you holding back from him? Ask God to illuminate your life with his light, and throw open wide the shutters of your heart. Ask him to come in, and make him welcome as your guest and master.

Or imagine a giant hydroelectric system, like the Hoover Dam. Think of the enormous power of countless millions of gallons of water cascading down to drive the great generators which give power to nearby cities. That power is available at the throw of a switch. It can be yours. You don't have to generate it yourself: that has been done for you. It is something on which you can rely. But you must make connection with it. Think of your repentance and acceptance of God's forgiveness as being like throwing a switch, thus allowing power to surge into your life. Have you thrown that switch? If so, all else has been done for you and you can rest assured that God is working within your life, slowly but surely. To be a Christian is to trust in the promises of God and be obedient to him. You may not feel that God is present—but your feelings are not necessarily reliable. This point is so important that we shall consider it in more detail now.

I don't experience God as being present in my life

Many Christians, especially those who have experienced a dramatic conversion experience, begin with a very strong sense of God's closeness. God seems very near and very real. The whole world seems to vibrate with his presence. There is a sense in which all of creation seems to tingle with the glory of God. After a while, however, this experience of the presence of God begins to wane. For some Christians God is no longer experienced as present. Doubt begins to settle in. Perhaps you feel anxious about the validity of that initial experience. Was it all just an emotional release without any real substance?

There are many things that need to be said in response to such an anxiety. To begin with, let's look at a great biblical event that illustrates very well the point involved. Think about the exodus from Egypt when Israel broke free from its Egyptian bondage, crossed the Red Sea, and began its long pilgrimage to the promised land. In the early days of the Exodus God was obviously

71

active and present. The pillars of cloud and fire were visible symbols and reminders of the presence and power of the Lord among his people (Exodus 13:20–21). The crossing of the Red Sea (Exodus 14) confirmed this. But soon discontent set in. Those who had been set free from bondage began to doubt the Lord, and demanded that he be put to the test. Was he *really* there? Was the long journey worth all the effort? Did God know what he was doing? As the march through the desert wilderness continued year after year, doubts grew stronger. They no longer experienced the presence of God. Of course, as any reader of the remainder of the Old Testament can hardly have failed to notice, God was indeed present during that period of wandering in the wilderness. With the triumphant entry into the promised land, the people's confidence in the Lord was fully restored and their doubts in the wilderness revealed for what they were. But think of yourself being in their situation in the wilderness. To start with, God seemed very close and his presence could hardly be ignored. But as the years wore on the memory of that early period seemed unreliable. Perhaps it was just imagined. God didn't seem to be present any more. You can understand how they felt—but how *unreliable* those feelings turned out to be! God had promised to be present with his people, wherever they went. That promise was and is grounded in the faithfulness of God, not in our subjective impressions of whether God is there or not!

In your early days as a Christian, you may have known a spiritual equivalent to those pillars of cloud and fire— an experience, a feeling of the presence and power of God. There may have been something like the parting of the Red Sea when God confirmed that he was really present and active in your life—perhaps an answered prayer, perhaps some kind of sign. Maybe that was some time ago. Now you may feel doubtful about your early feelings. But can you see how unreliable feelings are in deciding whether God is there or not? Or whether he cares for you or not? Or whether he knows what he is doing? Christianity is firmly grounded in the faithfulness of God to his promises, not in our feelings! Like Israel, you may find that something happens that restores your experience of the presence of God.

Experience depends as much on your mental state as on the way things really are. It is perfectly possible for these two statements to be true at one and the same time:

- God is there.
- I don't experience God as being there.

No contradiction is involved. One of the most moving descriptions of the feeling that God is not there is to be found in Psalm 42. The psalmist here speaks as someone in the depths of spiritual despair. He is downcast, dispirited, and anxious. He feels far from God. His friends have noticed this and make fun of him. "Where's this God of yours, then?" Yet despite this, he knows that God is still there. He remembers the good times, the times when he was close to God and knew it, and he takes enormous comfort from the knowledge—grounded in his confidence in the absolute faithfulness and trustworthiness of God—that this time of depression and despair will pass. The Psalm ends with a note of faith, even of triumph: "Put your hope in God, for I will yet praise him, my Savior and my God" (v. 11).

Notice what the psalmist does *not* do. He doesn't

73

pretend that his feelings of doubt and anxiety do not exist. Instead, he acknowledges them, and brings them before the Lord. He knows that, despite his feelings, God is still there. His feelings are like a cloud that passes in front of the sun and temporarily cuts off its light. Soon though the cloud does pass, and the sun once more comes into view.

Remember that it isn't just you who have experienced this sense of the absence of God all on your own. This isn't something new. It isn't something that has never happened before. And it doesn't mean that you're a lousy Christian. For example, the sense of the absence of God is a frequent theme in the writings of Martin Luther (the great German Reformer) and John of the Cross (a Spanish spiritual writer of the sixteenth century). You can turn to writers like these, who draw on their own experience and the experience of the people they've counseled, as they affirm God's total faithfulness to his promises, despite the temporary feeling of his absence. Take some comfort from the thought that many other Christians have had these feelings before you, and have gone on to tell of how they resolved them.

An excellent example of this is provided by Psalm 13. The Psalm opens with the psalmist expressing his deep and despondent sense of the absence of God. "How long, O Lord? Will you forget me forever? How long will you hide your face from me? How long must I wrestle with my thoughts and every day have sorrow in my heart?" (vv. 1–2). Perhaps you can identify with his position, sympathizing with his sadness at the feeling of God's absence. Perhaps you are experiencing such feelings even now. However, instead of becoming increasingly introverted, contemplating his own state of anxiety, the psalmist turns to contemplate the character of God: his trustworthiness, his covenant faithfulness, and his loving kindness. The Psalm thus ends with a sense of hope and expectation. "But I trust in your unfailing love; my heart rejoices in your salvation. I will sing to the Lord, for he has been good to me" (vv. 5–6).

Note how the psalmist turns to praise at this point. Praise can help throw off the sense of gloom that sometimes comes with doubt. Note also the decisive turn *away* from feelings *toward* the promises and character of God himself. It's very easy to get trapped in a rut of depression. You keep looking inward, examining your feelings and emotions and allow these to determine your spiritual state. Instead, you should turn outward, away from your feelings, and contemplate the promises of a trustworthy and faithful God that culminated in the death and resurrection of Jesus Christ. "For no matter how many promises God has made, they are 'Yes' in Christ" (2 Corinthians 1:20). Turn outward to other people, who can set your anxieties in perspective.

Finally, remember the advice that Screwtape gave his nephew Wormwood in the sixth *Screwtape* Letter. The best way to make Christians into atheists is to stop them thinking about *God*, and get them thinking about their own *states of mind about God*! Get them hopelessly preoccupied with their feelings and doubts, and stop them turning to God. Make them wallow in their uncertainties, so that they get despondent and discouraged. As C. S. Lewis knew, the certainty and security of the presence of God can easily be displaced by near-total doubt simply by fixing your attention on your mental state rather than on God himself.

I feel so inadequate as a Christian

Don't we all! When you consider the enormous responsibility and challenge of being a Christian, it's hardly surprising if you feel overwhelmed by it all. On the one hand, there is the task of proclaiming the gospel to the world for which Christ died. On the other, there is the task of ensuring that the love of God is expressed in lifestyles and programs of social and political action. The love of God draws us out of the world, only to send us back into it, as we try to transform the world in the light of the vision provided by the gospel.

Perhaps we feel rather like Joshua, as he stood poised on the frontiers of the promised land and contemplated the awesome responsibility that had just been placed upon his shoulders. Moses, the great man who had led Israel out of Egypt and through the wilderness, was dead; he, Joshua, had been chosen by God, and entrusted with the task of leading his people into the promised land (Joshua 1:1–5). Joshua must have felt very inadequate in the face of such a challenge. But being given responsibilities by God carries with it the promise of being given assistance by God. It isn't as if God tells us to do something incredibly difficult and leaves us to get on with it on our own. God's gifts are tailored to God's demands. Anyway, God knows our weaknesses and our abilities and matches his demands to those abilities. God's words to Joshua contain both command and promise—the command to lead his people into the promised land, and the promise that he, the living God, will be present with Joshua, sustaining and supporting him wherever he goes. "Have I not commanded you? Be strong and courageous. Do not be terrified; do not be discouraged, for the Lord your God will be with you wherever you go" (Joshua 1:9).

Or think of the apostles in those hectic days after the resurrection of Jesus. Only eleven in number, they were solemnly charged with the task of making disciples of all nations (Matthew 28:18–20). Imagine eleven people being told that they had to go and convert the whole world! You could understand if they felt a sense of despair, disbelief, and total inadequacy. "Eleven of us against the world? You must be kidding!" Yet the reality of the situation was actually rather different: it was eleven of them *and the living God* against the world. Jesus told the apostles not to attempt anything until they had received "the gift [which] my Father promised" (Acts 1:4; see also John 16:33). Their task required special divine assistance, which was duly provided at the first Pentecost, when God poured out his life-giving and enabling Spirit upon the apostles (Acts 2:1–12). Once more, God matched the needs of the situation to his gifts.

The basic pattern that emerges here is that of God who enables ordinary and inadequate people to achieve their calling. The same pattern is repeated in the lives of Christians down the centuries, and it can be in yours as well. Try reading the biographies of some famous Christians. Try reading the stories of some of the great missionaries and evangelists and see how God works in their lives. God bestows gifts to enable them to meet their challenges and opportunities in his service. As we survey the enormous tasks that confront the modern church, and try to determine what contribution we can make, it is important to realize that we are not working unaided. We are, to use Paul's wonderful phrase, "coworkers with God." Yet we are not equal partners, sharing the load evenly: it is God who plays the major part. Do your best—trust in God to do the rest. "The one who calls you is faithful, and he will do it" (1 Thessalonians 5:24).

God uses you—but, in the end, he doesn't depend on you. The graveyards of the world are full of people who imagined that the success of the gospel depended on them—yet the grave could not hold the one upon whom that success *really* depends. It is not us, but the risen Christ who sustains the gospel that we proclaim. See yourself as a channel through which the power and activity of the risen Christ can be directed into the world. It's not what you are that matters—it's what you let God do with you and through you!

Some Christians are crippled or depressed by a feeling of uselessness. They feel that they are worthless. But God's love *affirms* our personal worth, yet does not *depend* on our worthiness or merit. "Sinners are attractive because they are loved; they are not loved because they are attractive" (Martin Luther). Think of the overwhelming love of God shown for you in the death of Christ on the cross. See God affirming your personal worth. You are so important to God that Christ died for *you*. You matter to God—that is why he has chosen and called you.

Some Christians, however, suffer from a sense of spiritual pride that leads them to trust more and more in their own abilities and rely less and less upon the Lord. If this is the case, an awareness or recognition of your personal inadequacy can be an excellent asset. If you know that your trust in God is inadequate, you are less likely to have delusions about being able to manage by yourself, and so you can learn to turn to the Lord in prayer and expectation. You look to him for inspiration, guidance, and empowering. Being a Christian is a bit like being an electric motor: you need an external source of power. If you get disconnected from it, you're not much use!

Jesus used a more powerful analogy to make the same point: Christians are like branches on a vine (John 15:1–8). If the branch gets cut off the vine it withers away. It can only survive, and will only bear fruit, if it remains firmly attached to the vine and is able to draw on life-giving sap. The branch is not independent, but relies totally upon the vine for its life and its purpose— to yield fruit. Apart from Christ, we can do nothing— and a sense of our own inadequacy prevents us from getting the idea that we can do much of anything without turning to him. The gospel stresses that we must be receptive toward God, awaiting the gifts that he will give us to equip us for the tasks ahead.

Humility, then, is a very important virtue for a Christian. But humility is very easily misunderstood. If there is one thing that humility *isn't*, it is pretending that you have no special gifts or talents. (You might find it helpful to pray through Romans 12:3–8 or 1 Corinthians 12:4–11 alone or with a friend, asking for guidance on what gifts you possess.) Some Christians seem to think that to be humble you need to deny that you have any talents. This isn't humility—it's false modesty! Humility is about recognizing that our gifts and talents, whatever and however many they may be, are gifts of God, which owe nothing to our personal worthiness and owe everything to his generosity and loving kindness. "What do you have that you did not receive?" (1 Corinthians 4:7). The parable of the talents (Matthew 25:14–30) makes this point especially well.

The parable tells of a master who entrusts his money to some servants during his absence, and of the variety of ways in which the servants make use of that money. There are three main points being made by this parable.

Our talents are gifts from God. The servants had no claim on the money: it was their master's, entrusted to them during his absence. In one sense, it was a gift to them—but a gift that they would eventually have to surrender. They were stewards, rather than possessors, of the money. They were responsible for its wise use during the master's absence. In much the same way, we have been entrusted with gifts from God—not because of our personal worthiness, but because of the tasks and responsibilities that God may have in mind for us. None of us is totally devoid of talents however modest we may be about them. The important thing is to identify what your particular gifts might be, as the first step in using them in God's service. Many people pray to know the will of God in their lives without realizing that his gifts to us can express his will for us! If your gifts happen to meet real needs somewhere in the world, it's quite possible that's where God wants you to be. Identifying the gifts that God has given you is a useful way of beginning to discern God's will for your life.

How can you do this? Some talents are obvious. For example, you might be a very efficient organizer, a patient listener, or an accomplished musician. You will be aware of such talents yourself and be challenged to think through how you can use them to further the kingdom of God. Very often, however, personal gifts and talents are best discerned by others. It might be worth your while to talk this through with some close friends who can speak frankly about you. In addition to discovering what you *are* good at, you may also discover what you *aren't* good at! And don't be ashamed if your gifts turn out to be very ordinary and apparently unspectacular. As Paul emphasized, the Christian body needs a wide variety of members and gifts if it is to function (1 Corinthians 12:12–31). It's not up to us to ask why we have a certain gift, whatever it may be: the important thing is to ask what we can do with it in the service of the gospel. It's not what you have that matters—it's what you let God do with it. What you are is God's gift to you; what you become is your gift to God.

God's gifts are given in order to be used. You mustn't think of God's gifts as some kind of ornament, there just to decorate you and make you a more interesting person! They are there to be used in the building up of the people of God and in the furthering of his kingdom. In the parable of the talents, the returning master is furious with the servant who buried his talent and refused to use it. Some Christians adopt this ostrich-like approach to their gifts and talents, ignoring them or failing to use them. The English writer of the nineteenth century, John Henry Newman, suggested that each of us should think of ourselves as having to do something for God that nobody else could do. This is a very helpful thought. Identifying what gifts and talents we might have is one of the first steps in finding out what this "something" might be. But being prepared to *use* those gifts is essential! They are task-oriented, there for a purpose. They are all on loan. We are responsible for expending them in the world and we will be held accountable for the way in which we use them.

God's gifts increase through being used. The parable tells of three servants, two of whom use their talents, and the third who buries it in the ground. The buried talent remained unaltered in its hole in the ground. It was not used and therefore did not grow. The two other servants, however, found that the money with which they had been entrusted increased through being used wisely. And so it is with the gifts that God gives us— gifts such as faith. Faith increases by being used, by being put into action in God's service. Faith does not deepen by being allowed to stagnate, but by being applied.

In this respect, doubt is a positive thing. It is a stimulus to growth in faith. It snaps us out of our complacency. Like an alarm bell, it indicates that all is not well. Perhaps we have been like the third servant and have buried our faith in a hole in the ground and have failed to use it. Faith, like a plant, is something that is meant to grow. So *use* your faith. Allow it to affect the way you think and the way you live. Don't let it get neglected through disuse!

I'm a failure: What use can I be to God?

All of us fail God; not all of us, however, are willing to admit this. So let's begin on a positive note: your sense of failure points to your honesty and insight. C. S. Lewis once drew attention to one of the greatest paradoxes of human existence. We have enormously high ideals— that we fail to meet. Even knowing what is right and good, we seem unable to achieve these ideals in our lives. Many Christians find this paradox expressed in their lives: the deeper their faith, the greater their realization of their sinfulness and inadequacy. The closer they come to God the further they feel from him. The more they become aware of the overwhelming love of God for them, the more they realize just how little they love God in return. As a result, a sense of inadequacy and failure often arises from a deep awareness of the holiness and righteousness of the God who has called us. This in turn impresses on us the enormity of the moral gulf between ourselves and God. But this isn't really a sense of *failure*: if anything, it's a proper sense of perspective.

It is certainly true that many Christians are failures according to the standards of the world. Paul made this point forcefully when writing to the Corinthian church: "Brothers, think of what you were when you were called. Not many of you were wise by human standards; not many were influential; not many were of noble birth. But God chose the foolish things of the world to shame the wise; God chose the weak things of the world to shame the strong" (1 Corinthians 1:26–27; cf. 2 Corinthians 13:4). Success in the world usually comes by being assertive and aggressive, by ensuring that you come out on top in any conflict, and by destroying the reputations of your opponents. Wealth and power are seen as reasonable goals. The weak are legitimate victims of the strong. The gospel, however, specifies a somewhat different lifestyle—a lifestyle that seems sheer stupidity to those who judge by worldly standards. Great stress is placed on care and compassion for others, especially the weak. Selfish attitudes and behavior are discouraged. The well-being of others is placed above personal success. It is impossible to read the

Sermon on the Mount (Matthew 5–7) and avoid seeing areas of serious conflict between Christ's teaching and modern Western business and social ethics.

I was once travelling from London to Geneva in Switzerland and found myself having to spend a long time at London's Heathrow Airport. The flight had been delayed because of fog. I must admit that I find airports rather boring places, and to relieve my boredom, I picked up a copy of the local airport magazine. One of its articles fascinated me. "How *you* can become a successful business executive!" I sat down to read it. It was mainly about how to develop manipulative techniques and project the image of domination and competence. Part of the article was a questionnaire. One question was, "When you are in a meeting, what is your aim in reaching a decision?" I looked at the various options, and circled "to reach the decision which benefits most people." The right answer was "to come out on top"! After a while, I began to realize that I just didn't have what it took to be a successful business executive—at least by the standards of that magazine— and felt really glad that I didn't! A really "successful" and powerful business executive or corporate lawyer may seem to have conquered the world when in reality he or she has been conquered by the world.

Many Christians unwittingly carry these secular standards of success over into their lives as believers. They still think of "success" in terms laid down by the world. "Success" means an ability to dominate and manipulate others, to get to the top by any means available, to have status and power. As a result, it is hardly surprising that they judge themselves and many other Christians to be failures! But what standards are being used here? The

84

gospel challenges the values of the world. It affirms the existence and importance of a different set of values—the values of the kingdom of God. These values are reflected in the lives of Christians who will inevitably find themselves in tension with at least some of the standards and values of the world. The world says: "Seek money, status, and possessions." The gospel says: "Seek first the kingdom of God." To become a Christian is to adopt a new lifestyle and a new set of values that the world may well brand as ludicrous. But does what the world thinks really matter?

Some Christians, however, are acutely aware of having failed God on some specific occasion, or even on a whole series of occasions. Perhaps you feel guilty because you know you could have served God better than you did. Perhaps you failed to speak to someone about the gospel. Perhaps you hurt a friend because of what you said or did. Perhaps you did something that you know to have been wrong. You feel that you are a failure in God's sight. What could he conceivably do through you?

The answer is quite simple: a lot! The classic example of a failure is Peter. Peter, you will remember, was the disciple who utterly failed Jesus when the going got really tough. In Gethsemane, Peter had affirmed that he would never let Jesus down. "Even if I have to die with you, I will never disown you" (Matthew 26:35). Brave words—but, as events showed, hollow ones. Shortly afterward, when Jesus had been arrested, Peter was approached by a servant girl in the high priest's courtyard. "You were with Jesus of Nazareth," she said. Here was an opportunity for Peter to witness to his loyalty to Jesus! However, Peter panicked. If words

85

ever amounted to an admission of total failure, the words of Peter are a prime example, "I don't know what you're talking about!. . .I don't know the man!" (Matthew 26:69–75).

Yet at the heart of the gospel are the themes of forgiveness and renewal. God forgives our past failings and empowers us to start afresh. Martin Luther once described the Christian life as "a kind of beginning all over again." The past may be set behind us as God forgives us for our past failings and empowers us to overcome future failings. After Jesus' resurrection, Peter became a changed man. No longer was he a coward who sought to deny Jesus, but a potential martyr who was prepared to proclaim his Savior to the ends of the earth. It is generally thought that Peter was finally crucified in Rome during the Neronian persecutions in A.D. 65— finally and triumphantly sharing the fate of his Lord.

See your own failings reflected in the light of Peter's. Perhaps you thought you could cope with the pressures of a situation only to discover that you couldn't. And you felt that you let the Lord down. It's not the first time it has happened to anyone. Peter must have felt much the same way as you: he was reduced to tears when he realized what a failure he had been (Matthew 26:75). But that was not the end of Peter's story, nor should it be the end of *your* story. If you feel that you have let God down, tell him so. Take it to him in prayer. "Trust the past to the mercy of God, the present to his love, the future to his providence" (St. Augustine). There is no need to tell anyone else. Remember that God already knows what you have done and how you feel about it (Psalm 139:1–6), so you don't need to hide your fears and anxieties from him. Ask him for forgiveness, and for wisdom and strength to cope with such situations in the future. And when you finish praying, do so with the confidence of one who has been forgiven, ready to face the challenges and opportunities awaiting you.

For all their unfaithfulness and imperfection, God is willing to use his people and to do great things through them. Indeed, it is hard to say which is more remarkable—that people should be so unfaithful, or that God should be able to work so marvelously through their unfaithfulness. The sinfulness and pettiness of individuals, the blind selfishness of the churches, the niggardliness of the support that has been given to the work of the gospel, the mistakes that have been made—all point to the weakness and failure of people like us. And yet the church survives, the body of Christ in every land, the great miracle of history in which the living God himself through his Holy Spirit is pleased to dwell. God is able to work through human failures, including yours. Indeed, failure makes us less likely to trust in our own judgment and abilities, and instead to rely upon the Lord. This insight is central to Paul's understanding of our life as Christians. "[God] said to me, 'My grace is sufficient for you, for my power is made perfect in weakness.' Therefore I will boast all the more gladly about my weaknesses, so that Christ's power may rest on me" (2 Corinthians 12:9). So don't be anxious if you feel that you are a failure, or that you are totally inadequate as a Christian. The real problems start if you think you're a success, or if you begin to think you're capable of leading a brilliantly successful Christian life trusting in your own strength. The God who has called *you* is a God who makes his strength perfect through human weakness. Let's be honest: we're *all* failures when it comes to being Christians. That's why it's such wonderful news that God is able to work through (even despite!) our failures, comforting and reassuring us before sending us out to try again.

Questions for discussion

- In what ways is doubt linked with a sense of personal inadequacy?
- How would you go about identifying your gifts and talents?
- What do you feel your main weaknesses are? Are they an obstacle to God, or an opportunity for him?
- What criteria of "success" are appropriate for the Christian?

Doubts about Jesus

Chapter 4

Doubts about Jesus

Doubts about Jesus tend to be very factual. Every now and then, television or radio features appear that claim to have radical new evidence that totally discredits the Christian understanding of Jesus. Such sensationalist items may help attract large audiences; but, their scholarly content is generally low and their alleged conclusions forgotten within weeks. Some Christians, however, find that serious doubts have been raised in their minds. They do not have access to the scholarly material on which these programs claim to be based and so tend to treat their claims as credible. Thus, the present chapter thus deals with the main doubts which are likely to arise in relation to the history of Jesus.

Did Christians get Jesus wrong?

A number of doubts might arise in this context. Very often, books are published with sensational come-ons— "the explosively controversial international best-seller," for example. These books claim to have recovered "suppressed evidence" concerning Jesus. They allege that Christians hushed up facts about Jesus that didn't fit in with their ideas. Sometimes these claims cause Christians some anxiety; however, as we shall suggest, these anxieties are needless.

One such doubt might be whether Jesus really existed. In fact, the grounds for suggesting that he did not are astonishingly flimsy. Only someone who had already made up their mind that Jesus did not exist as an historical individual could approach the evidence and come to the conclusion that he did not exist. If the existence of Jesus is to be denied on the basis of the evidence available, we would be obliged to deny the existence of an alarming number of historical individuals! Although doubts may be raised on this matter by your friends, or hostile critics of Christianity, the evidence is strongly against them. An example of this type of work is a book written by John Allegro, a hitherto respected scholar, who argued that the word "Jesus" was nothing more and nothing less than some sort of code word for a sacred mushroom that produced hallucinations in those who consumed them. The early Christians, he argued, far from being worshipers of Jesus Christ, were secret mushroom eaters.

The evidence brought forward was quite inadequate. Apart from destroying Allegro's reputation as a serious scholar, the book pointed to how easy it was to gain public attention for a theory that suggested Jesus *wasn't* what Christians have claimed him to be, and how difficult it is to draw attention to the refutation of such theories by Christians. To claim to have sensational new evidence to disprove Christianity generates a lot of publicity and helps sell the book or advertising space on the television feature in question. But the Christian side of the argument is generally not heard. It lacks novelty value. It's not newsworthy.

The suggestion that Christianity may have gotten Jesus wrong has been thoroughly explored over the last two hundred years. Just about every possibility has been given careful weight. Jesus might have been a radical vegetarian, a failed revolutionary, a misguided prophet, or perhaps nothing more than a religious teacher of common sense. The first Christians might even have deliberately distorted him at points. All these possibilities have been given careful scholarly consideration, yet none has been shown to have any real plausibility.

In the nineteenth century, a movement known as the "Quest of the Historical Jesus" got under way, aiming to show that the New Testament suppressed a picture of Jesus that Christians didn't like. Although this movement can still be detected today, it has lost most of its intellectual credibility. It has been given full scholarly attention, and has been found wanting. Behind these allegedly historical "reconstructions" of Jesus may be detected a web of questionable historical scholarship and vested interests. "Rediscovered Jesuses" tended to look remarkably like their rediscoverers! In his essay "Fern-seed and Elephants," C. S. Lewis writes as follows on "rediscovered Jesuses":

> All theology of the liberal type involves at some point—and very often involves throughout—the claim that the real behaviour and purpose and teaching of Christ came very rapidly to be misunderstood and misrepresented by his followers, and has been recovered or exhumed only by modern scholars. Now long before I became interested in

theology I had met this kind of theory elsewhere. . . . One was brought up to believe that the real meaning of Plato had been misunderstood by Aristotle, and wildly travestied by the neo-Platonists, only to be recovered by the moderns. When recovered, it turned out (most fortunately) that Plato had really all along been an English Hegelian, rather like T. H. Green. I have met it a third time in my own professional studies; every week or so a clever undergraduate, every quarter a dull American don, discovers for the first time what some Shakespearian play really meant.

Is the resurrection some sort of cover-up job?

One doubt which often arises is whether the resurrection really happened, or whether it was some kind of cover-up job to conceal the real fate of Jesus. This suggestion was made frequently in the eighteenth century and is still encountered today. Doubts about the resurrection arise from suggestions of this kind, along with the deep-down feeling of some Christians—that the resurrection is just too good to be true!

For example, some Christians experience anxiety over the resurrection because of a feeling that can be expressed along the following lines. It was easy for the first Christians to believe in the resurrection of Jesus. After all, belief in resurrections was commonplace at the time. The first Christians may have jumped to the conclusion that Jesus was raised from the dead when something rather different actually happened. In fact, however, neither of the two contemporary beliefs of the time bear any resemblance to the resurrection of Jesus. The Sadducees denied the idea of a resurrection altogether (a fact that Paul was able to exploit at an awkward moment: Acts 23:6–8) while the majority expected a general resurrection on the last day, at the end of history itself.

The sheer oddness of the Christian proclamation of the resurrection of Jesus in human history, at a definite time and place, is all too easily overlooked today even though it was obvious at the time. The unthinkable appeared to have happened, and for that very reason demanded careful attention. Far from merely fitting into the popular expectation of the pattern of resurrection, what happened to Jesus actually contradicted it. The sheer novelty of the Christian position at the time has been obscured by two thousand years' experience of the Christian understanding of the resurrection. We've become used to the idea of Jesus being raised from the dead—yet *at the time* it was wildly unorthodox and radical. The resurrection of Jesus simply did not conform to contemporary expectations. It wasn't what was expected at all. In fact, so strange is that idea that we have to give a convincing explanation to account for it. That explanation is provided by the resurrection as an historical event.

Of course some critics have suggested, on Freudian grounds, that the resurrection of Jesus is explicable as some kind of wish fulfillment on the part of the disciples. This also strains the imagination somewhat. Why should the disciples have responded to the catastrophe of Jesus' death by making the hitherto unprecedented suggestion that he had been raised from the dead? The history of Israel is littered with the corpses of pious Jewish martyrs, none of whom were ever thought of as having been raised from the dead in such a manner. Furthermore, many of the disciples (such as

Peter and Paul) appear to have been martyred for their faith: why die for a lie?

If you are anxious about the resurrection, you may find some of the following points helpful. (They by no means exhaust the evidence for the resurrection—for that you should consult the works listed at the end of the book. Nevertheless, they are useful pointers to guide your thinking.)

1. Note the emphasis on the historical fact common to all four Gospels: the tomb was empty (Matthew 28:1–10; Mark 16:1–8; Luke 24:1–11; John 20:1–9). This doesn't prove the resurrection—but it is consistent with it. The Gospels build up an overall picture of the events of the first Easter Day—each account falls into place like a piece in a jigsaw puzzle—consistent with the others and giving a total picture of what happened.

2. The practice of "tomb veneration" was common in New Testament times. In other words, the tomb of a prophet was used by his disciples as a place of worship. Matthew 23:29–30 almost certainly refers to this practice, which continues to this day: the tomb of David in Jerusalem is still venerated by many Jews. But there is no record whatsoever of any such veneration of the tomb of Jesus by his disciples. Why not? The simple fact was that Jesus' body was disquietingly missing from its tomb.

There seems to have been no dispute about this at the time. The rumor of Jesus' resurrection could have been suppressed without the slightest difficulty by the authorities simply by publicly displaying his corpse. It is of the greatest importance that the New Testament does not contain as much as a hint of any attempt to explain away the existence of Jesus' corpse. Nor is there any hint that the Jewish authorities either produced, or attempted to produce, this corpse. Had this been done, the preaching of the early church would have been discredited immediately. But it wasn't. All the evidence indicates that the tomb was empty on the third day. The controversy at the time concerned not the fact of the empty tomb, but the explanation of that emptiness.

3. Within a very short period after his death, Jesus was being described in remarkably exalted terms by his followers. Jesus was not venerated as a dead prophet or rabbi, but was worshiped as the living and risen Lord. At some points in the New Testament, Jesus appears to be explicitly identified with God himself. At several points in the New Testament, words originally referring to God himself are applied to Jesus. For example, in Romans 10:13 Paul says that "everyone who calls upon the name of the Lord [Jesus, in this case] will be saved"—yet the original of this Old Testament quotation (Joel 2:32) is actually a statement to the effect that everyone who calls upon the name of *God* will be saved.

But how could this remarkable transformation in the perceived status of Jesus who died as a common criminal have come about? If he was a prophet, or maybe even a martyr, the most we could expect would be veneration of his tomb (see Matthew 23:29). Why then did the early Christians start talking about a dead rabbi as if he were God? And, perhaps even more intriguing, why did they start talking about him as if he was alive, praying to him and worshiping him? Taken on its own, this argument proves little; taken in conjunction with all the other pointers, it helps build up a consistent and convincing picture of the resurrection event.

How can someone who lived two thousand years ago be relevant to me?

This question causes difficulty and anxiety for some Christians. To deal with this anxiety, think of Jesus as an *event*, rather than just a *person*. Something *happened* through Jesus. God *made something possible* through Jesus. Think of Jesus as establishing the grounds of a renewed relationship with God, a new attitude to life, a new hope in the face of death. Or think of him as opening up the way home to God. For in dealing with Jesus we aren't dealing simply with a human being like ourselves, but with God himself, acting in history to redeem us. God chose to act through Jesus Christ, supremely through his death and resurrection, making available to us something that otherwise would not have been open to us. You can sense this excitement in the opening of 1 Peter, "Praise be to the God and Father of our Lord Jesus Christ. In his great mercy he has given us new birth into a living hope through the resurrection of Jesus Christ from the dead, and into an inheritance that can never perish, spoil or fade" (1 Peter 1:3–4).

In the first place, then, Jesus is of importance to the Christian faith in that, through his death and resurrection, he made possible a whole new way of living. Jesus is the ground of faith: it is on account of his obedience to the will of his father, supremely demonstrated in his suffering and death on the cross, that our new relationship to God is possible. The Cross is not just an event in history that took place some two thousand years ago: it is the foundation of our faith *now*. It is through the death of Jesus Christ that our new life is possible. "He himself bore our sins in his body on the tree, so that we

98

might die to sins and live for righteousness; by his wounds you have been healed" (1 Peter 2:24). Without the achievement of the Cross, redemption would not be a present possibility for us. Jesus is important because God achieves the salvation of sinful humanity through him. He is the agent of salvation, the one through whom God worked and still works.

In the second place, Jesus prompts people to ask questions; to begin thinking about God and themselves. Jesus once asked the disciples, "Who do *you* say that I am?" (Mark 8:29). That same question has caused many to ponder and wonder ever since. Christianity is not merely the teachings of Jesus, as Marxism is the teaching of Karl Marx, or Thatcherism the teaching of Margaret Thatcher. The gospel is not just *about* Jesus; it *is* Jesus. Christianity isn't just about *ideas*; it is about a *person*. For many people who subsequently become Christians, Jesus acts as a catalyst or a stimulant to their thinking. The long chain of thought that climaxes in repentance and acceptance of forgiveness often begins with interest in the person of Jesus.

There is something strangely attractive about Jesus, something that is able to reach across the gulf of history and intrigue people even today. Questions about Jesus soon become questions about God and salvation. "Who is Jesus?" easily becomes "How can I find a gracious God?" "Why did Jesus have to die?" gives way to "What must I do to be saved?" Interest in Jesus as a person is often the beginning of a long and secret process of reflection that eventually culminates in acceptance of him as Lord and Savior.

Finally, Jesus indicates what that redeemed life is like. Not only is he the foundation of the life of faith; but by his life, he shows us what shape or form the Christian life takes. He maps out a way of living appropriate for believers. His teaching points to the need to value God, to obey him, and to ensure that nothing comes before him. By his example, he helps us understand what obedience to God implies. He acts as a model for the sort of love that Christians should show to one another. Writing to the Thessalonian Christians, Paul speaks of how, through their conversion, they "became imitators of us and of the Lord" (1 Thessalonians 1:6). Being a Christian means being "conformed to the likeness of [God's] son" (Romans 8:29), a process in which God graciously makes us more like Jesus as we deepen in our faith and obedience. So the fact that Jesus lived two thousand years ago does not diminish his relevance to the life of faith. Without what Jesus achieved, a life of faith and all that it implies would not be possible. Our faith, our hope, all that matters to us—these are all the consequence of what God achieved for us through Jesus. The fact that this new life is a present possibility for others rests upon the solid foundation of Jesus Christ. In evangelism, we proclaim that the death and resurrection of Jesus makes possible and makes available a new way of living, a way of living charged with the knowledge of forgiveness and the hope of resurrection and eternal life. That process may be described as "being conformed to Christ," so that we become more like him in the way we behave. Both the foundation and the shape of the redeemed life are built upon Jesus—in New Testament times, and today. Through the power of the Holy Spirit, God conforms us to the likeness of his Son who lives and reigns within us—not as one from the dim and distant past, but as the risen and present Lord.

Questions for discussion

- Why do "rediscovered Jesuses" tend to resemble those who rediscover them?
- Is it possible to prove that Jesus was raised from the dead?
- Why is Jesus so important to the Christian faith?

Doubts about God

Chapter 5

Doubts about God

Finally, we turn to consider some anxieties about God himself. In an aggressively secular society, such as modern western Europe or North America, it is very easy for a Christian—especially one who has come to faith recently—to feel threatened and insecure. Is God really there when so many people deny his existence? Is my faith based upon a delusion or a logical error? Unease over such questions is natural, and it is hoped that the response given here may be helpful.

Anxieties about God, however, concern more than his existence. Is he faithful to his promises? Does he really love me, a sinner? These questions trouble many Christians, especially when they go through some kind of spiritual dry spell (quite a common occurrence, by the way: cf. Psalm 63:1). Although we have already looked at some doubts about God (for example, when you don't experience God as being present in your life), the additional material presented here should help you think and pray through your worries.

Is God really there?

There are no knock-down arguments that irrefutably establish God's existence, just as there are none that decisively disprove it. Whether people believe or disbelieve in God, their position is a matter of faith, not fact. It may be a fact that God is an irrelevance to many individuals, just as it may be a fact that many people do not believe in God—but this does not mean that it is a fact that God does not exist. But faith in God doesn't depend on an argument anyway. The Austrian philosopher Ludwig Wittgenstein remarked that he'd never met anyone who came to faith in God on account of an argument! Rather, arguments for God's existence are developed as back-up defenses for the gospel for the benefit of those who think this is important. Some people need to be reassured that Christianity makes sense; arguments for the existence of God show that a rational case can indeed be made for belief in him. By the end of this chapter it will be obvious that God's existence doesn't depend on those arguments—but it can be helpful to know that a case can be made for it.

In the end, however, we know that God exists (and who and what he is) because he has revealed himself. Arguments for the existence of God may help prepare the way for this revelation (Romans 1:18–20), but they are no substitute for it. If Christianity was about our search for God, there would be permanent difficulties in agreeing on who or what God was, let alone whether he existed. Different search parties would come back from their expeditions with differing reports, unable to reach agreement on their results.

Christianity, however, affirms that God has come

looking for us. His existence is disclosed by his search for us, and ultimately by his encounter with us. C. S. Lewis wrote powerfully of the profound *silliness* of the idea of "our search for God" in his work *Miracles*.

The Pantheist's God does nothing, demands nothing. He is there if you wish for him, like a book on a shelf. He will not pursue you. . . .The shock comes at the precise moment when the thrill of *life* is communicated to us along the clue we have been following. It is always shocking to meet life when we thought we were alone. . . . And therefore this is the very point at which many draw back—I would have done so myself if I could—and proceed no further with Christianity. An "impersonal God"—well and good. A subjective God of beauty, truth and goodness, inside our own heads—better still. A formless life-force surging through us, a vast power which we can tap—best of all. But God himself, alive, pulling at the other end of the cord, perhaps approaching at infinite speed, the hunter, king, husband—that is quite another matter. There comes a moment when the children who have been playing at burglars hush suddenly: was that a *real* footstep in the hall? There comes a moment when people who have been dabbling in religion ("Man's search for God"!) suddenly draw back. Supposing we really found him? We never meant to come to *that*! Worse still supposing he had found us?

In *Surprised by Joy*, Lewis further suggests that our alleged search for God is rather like the mouse who went out looking for the cat. "It is a dreadful thing to fall into the hands of the living God" (Hebrews 10:31)—it demands obedience, conversion and newness of life!

For many Christians, the sudden conversion of their friends (or even their own conversion) points to the existence of God. An individual who up to that point has been hostile to God suddenly changes. God suddenly becomes both meaningful and present to them. Something has happened. But what? And how? Throughout,

Scripture bristles with ideas and images which help illuminate this event, all pointing to the idea of an active God who discloses his existence not through *argument* but through *action*. The confrontation with Saul of Tarsus is perhaps the classic example of this. God suddenly becomes real in our experience.

It is interesting to notice that no biblical writer ever feels the need to prove the existence of God. That God *is* there is taken for granted. How could anyone think he wasn't? He was experienced and encountered; he made demands of individuals and communities; he promised to be with his people wherever they went. Thus the resurrection of Jesus is not taken by New Testament writers as a proof of the existence of God, but is interpreted as assigning Jesus a status equal with that of God. It is very difficult for someone who has experienced the power and presence of God to doubt that he exists.

Is God faithful to his promises?

Both Old and New Testaments affirm that God makes promises to us. Many of these promises are powerful and deeply moving. The great promise of God to Joshua is an inspiration to many Christians: "Be strong and courageous. Do not be terrified; do not be discouraged, for the Lord your God will be with you wherever you go" (Joshua 1:9). As Christians we must learn to trust in the gracious promises of God, promises such as that made to Joshua, and through him to us. But how reliable are these promises? How trustworthy is God? Christianity lays great stress on the total truthfulness and trustworthiness of God—but how well-placed is this trust? Is God faithful to his promises?

This question is one that perplexed many Jews shortly before the time of Jesus. God had promised them a Messiah. He had promised to come to his temple. He had promised to send his messenger before him to prepare the way for his coming (e.g. Malachi 3:1). But nothing had happened. Judea was under Roman occupation. Prophecy had died out. The word of the Lord was rarely heard in the land (as in the days of Eli: 1 Samuel 3:1). It seemed as if the great promises of God would come to nothing.

Then John the Baptist appeared in the country around Judea (Mark 1:1–8). It is difficult for the modern reader to understand the sense of excitement and expectation which this aroused. He was dressed like Elijah (Mark 1:6; cf. 2 Kings 1:8), the greatest of the prophets. He spoke with authority and proclaimed that he had come to prepare the way for the coming of God to his people. How the old Hebrew prophecies must have come to life again, as people swarmed across the Judean countryside to hear this remarkable man and speculate about who would follow him. Whose way had he prepared?

I remember once having to spend a damp winter Sunday afternoon waiting for a train to arrive at Nottingham station in the English east midlands. My wife and son had been to visit relatives in Chester, and were returning that afternoon. The train was due to arrive at 3:30. My faith in British railways has never been especially great, and it was lowered still further that afternoon. By 4:10 the train had still not arrived. Eventually there was an announcement. A rather despondent, disembodied female voice told us that British Rail regretted that the train had been delayed, but it should arrive in twenty minutes. I, and about fifty others, waited twenty minutes. It got dark, and the fog from the nearby canal enveloped the platform. People began to huddle up against each other for warmth. Nothing happened. Ten minutes later, another announcement was made. A decidedly gloomy voice told us that British Rail was very sorry, but there would be a delay of at least half an hour before the train arrived. The train was definitely on its way, but all sorts of problems had developed along the line. Finally, at 5:55, a decidedly more cheerful female voice announced that the train now approaching platform five was the delayed train from Chester. In other words, it had been sighted, and at any moment it would pull into the station. A cheer went up from the waiting crowd who clearly shared my frustration at having to spend the best part of a miserable Sunday afternoon in this way.

I imagine Israel felt much the same relief when John the Baptist appeared. He was like the voice who announced that a delayed train was just about to arrive. Something was happening and things were on the move. The long-awaited arrival of the Messiah was imminent. And just as the small crowd of us surged to the edge of the platform to catch a glimpse of the incoming train, so the Jews streamed out into the countryside to catch a glimpse of the long-awaited Messiah.

For the New Testament writers, the coming of God's Messiah to his people is one of the best demonstrations of God's faithfulness to his promises. For example, it's very difficult to read Matthew's gospel and miss his excitement at pointing out how great old prophecies found their fulfillment in Jesus. The same sort of excitement, even relief, can be seen in Simeon's over-

110

joyed reaction at seeing Jesus: at last, everything I have waited for from the Lord has come to pass! Now I can die with peace of mind (Luke 2:28–32). God had faithfully fulfilled his promises to his people.

For Paul, the faithfulness of God was of central importance. This faithfulness is demonstrated in the life, death, and resurrection of Jesus, in which the promises of the Old Testament are taken up and fulfilled. "For no matter how many promises God has made, they are 'Yes' in Christ" (2 Corinthians 1:20). The coming of Christ is seen as the fulfillment of the great Old Testament prophecies of God's coming to dwell among his people, just as the resurrection is seen as a fulfillment of God's promise of redemption. And on the basis of that faithfulness to his past promises, we may trust those that still await fulfillment—the great New Testament promises of renewal and eternal life.

It's helpful to think about the faith of the Old Testament saints at this point. They trusted passionately in the power of the Lord to redeem them. Yet, until the coming of Jesus Christ, the great divine promises of redemption seemed unfulfilled. But we can look back on the Old Testament period and see how those great promises were fulfilled through the coming of Jesus. In his life, his death, and his resurrection Jesus demonstrated God's faithfulness to his promises. It's much *easier* for us to believe in the promises of God than it was for the Old Testament saints—they never got to see those promises fulfilled in Jesus! Through Jesus, "we have the word of the prophets made more certain" (2 Peter 1:19): in other words, the great promises of the Old Testament are made more credible by the coming of Jesus.

111

One of the most powerful passages in the New Testament describes the nature of faith in God (Hebrews 11:1–12:3). In this passage, we are reminded of the deeds of many of the great figures of the Old Testament. Their faith in God and his gracious promises is shown in their actions. Abraham trusted in God and left his native land to go to the land chosen by God. Moses left Egypt in faith, trusting in the great promise of redemption. It was in these promises that the coming of Christ to redeem his people was anticipated. None of these great Old Testament believers saw the coming of Jesus—yet they placed their faith in the promises of God. "All these people were still living by faith when they died. They did not receive the things promised; they only saw them and welcomed them from a distance" (Hebrews 11:13). We have received what was promised to them—the coming of the Redeemer, Jesus Christ. We share their faith in the same God—but we can have greater confidence in his promises, because of their confirmation through the coming of Jesus.

More importantly, consider what we know about the character and purpose of God as we know it through the death of Jesus Christ on the cruel cross of Calvary for our salvation. In the death of Jesus upon that cross we learn that God loves sinners such as ourselves, that he is committed to the cause of our redemption. God shows his love for us, in that Christ died for us while we were still sinners (Romans 5:8). This is the God with whom we are dealing—the God who has given everything at his disposal to demonstrate his astonishing love for us, and bring us back to him. It is simply inconceivable that God, having invested so much in our well-being and care, having committed himself to us in word and deed, should abandon us or fail to be faithful to us. The cross of Christ demonstrates the vital fact that God stands by his promises, whatever the cost to himself, asking us to accept them, trust them, and thus to enter into eternal life with him—something that nothing, not even the very gates of Hell themselves, can tear away from us.

God is working his purpose out—and part of that purpose is the salvation of sinful human beings, people like you and me. If God is on our side, who is against us? Or, as the motto of Oxford University has it, "The Lord is my light and my salvation—whom shall I fear? The Lord is the stronghold of my life—of whom shall I be afraid?" (Psalm 27:1). Remind yourself of the words of reassurance spoken by Jesus to Nicodemus: "God so loved the world that he gave his one and only Son, that whoever believes in him shall not perish but have eternal life" (John 3:16). You may be reassured that God loves you, and that by putting your trust in him you enter into a relationship with him. The gospel is not about an easy ride through life; it makes hard and difficult demands of us. But it also makes us a promise— the promise of the presence and comfort of God as we seek to do his will in his world. And the comfort of knowing that God stands by us, even in our darkest hours, is more than I can ever hope to convey in print.

How can I know that God loves me?

This is a question that has troubled many Christians, especially those who are intensely aware of their own sinfulness. Somehow, it seems that God can only love us if he ignores our sin, or pretends that we aren't really sinners after all. Experience, conscience, and faith seem

113

to be out of step here! How can God love people like us?

Much the same point is made by Paul. It's conceivable that you might imagine circumstances under which you might give your life for somebody else. Of course, it would have to be somebody rather splendid, a really good person. Even then, however, it would still be unusual for someone to die for another person. Yet God demonstrates his love for us, in that Christ died for us while we were still sinners (Romans 5:6–8). What on earth would he do that for? Why should God love sinners so much? Even before we got around to repenting, God loved us. Amazingly, God loved us long before we loved him (1 John 4:10–11).

Our disbelief that God could love us ultimately rests on our feeling that God's love must depend on our attractiveness. We find it difficult to see anything special about ourselves that should merit so astonishing and so loving a response from God. But God's love for us ultimately rests on his own character. We have the privilege of being made in his image (Genesis 1:26–27). The Cross of Christ expresses the nature and the full extent of God's tender love for us, assuring us of how precious we are in his sight. How often has it been said that "Beauty is in the eye of the beholder"? Why should God see us as worthy of his love? Not because of anything that we have *done*, or anything that we *are*— but because of what God is like, and what he has done for us through Jesus Christ.

In part, our difficulty in accepting the fact that God loves us arises from a sense of sin. Most of us because of our selfishness and guilt feel profoundly unworthy of God's love. Sin profoundly affects what we think, say, and do. It tends to make us skeptical about God, disobedient to him, and reluctant to trust him. Yet God is able to distinguish between sin and the sinner. Sin is like a force that holds us captive against our will; God sees us as captives struggling to escape, and takes pity on us. Sin is like rust that distorts the image of God within us; God anticipates the renewal and restoration of that image. Sin is like a wound that disfigures us; God looks forward to the time when we will, through his grace, be healed. Sin is like a layer of dirt or corrosion that makes us seem unattractive and unbecoming; God sees us as washed clean, our beauty restored to what it was on the first morning of creation.

An illustration might be helpful here. In the late fifteenth century, the Florentine sculptor Agostino d'Antonio began work on a huge block of marble with a view to producing a spectacular sculpture. After a few futile attempts to make something out of it he gave it up as worthless. The block of marble—now badly disfigured—lay idle for forty years. Then Michelangelo took an interest in it. He saw beyond the ugly disfigured block of marble to the magnificent artistic creation he knew he could achieve with it. As a result, he began work. The final statue—the celebrated "David"—is widely regarded as one of the most outstanding artistic achievements of all time.

Michelangelo was able to see beyond the ugly exterior of the block of marble to what he could eventually achieve with it. Similarly, God is able to see beyond our sinful predicament and all its consequences, to knowing what he will be able to do with us by breaking the power of sin and restoring us to his image and likeness. Within each of us the image of God (Genesis 1:26–27) is found, however disfigured and corrupted by sin it may presently be. God is able to recover this image through grace as we are conformed to Christ. Just as the figure of "David" lay hidden within the marble, discernible only to the eye of its creator, so the image of God (however tarnished by sin) lies within us, seen and known by God himself. Yet God loves us *while* we are still sinners! He doesn't have to wait until we stop sinning! Acceptance of that love of God for us is a major step along the road that leads to our liberation from the tyranny of sin.

Finally, how can we be reassured of the love of God for us? Perhaps one of the most helpful ways of doing this is to reflect on the image of the dying Christ stretched out on the cross for us. Try to imagine the scene. Even better, find some paintings of the scene, such as those that have become classics in the history of art. Perhaps you could read one of the four Passion narratives (Matthew 27:11–65; Mark 15; Luke 23; John 18:28–19:42), and picture the events of that first Good Friday and Easter Day. Think carefully of the loneliness, of the pain, of the suffering, of the sense of hopelessness and helplessness of the scene. Think of that sad and dignified face contorted with pain. Let the full horror of that scene impress itself on your mind. And all of this was because God loved you and gave his only Son for you.

For many Christians, one of the most powerful ways of recalling this scene and understanding its relevance for us is to share in a communion service. The bread and the wine are visible, tangible reminders of that scene. They represent the sufferings of Christ. They are "dear tokens of his passion" (Charles Wesley). And as you eat and drink the bread and wine, you are being reminded of the enormous cost of your redemption, of how much you must matter to God because he went to such lengths to find you. Let the bread and wine act as triggers to your memory, starting off trains of thought that converge on the crucifixion of the Lord. "This is love: not that we loved God, but that he loved us and sent his Son as an atoning sacrifice for our sins" (1 John 4:10).

An aunt of mine died some time ago after having lived to be eighty or so. She had never married. During the course of clearing out her possessions, we came across a battered old photograph of a young man. My aunt had, it turned out, fallen hopelessly in love as a young girl. It had ended tragically. She never loved anyone else, and kept a photograph of this man she had loved for the remainder of her life. Why? Partly to remind herself that she had once been loved by someone. As she grew old, she knew that she would have difficulty in believing that, at one point in her life, she really had meant something to someone; that someone had once cared for her and regarded her as his everything. It could all have seemed a dream, an illusion, something she had invented in her old age to console her in her declining years—except that the photograph showed that to be untrue. It reminded her that her feelings had not been invented; she really had loved someone once, and was loved in return. The photograph was her sole link with a world in which she had been valued.

The communion bread and wine are like that photograph. They reassure us that something that seems too good to be true—something that we might even be suspected of having invented—really did happen. They are reminders of that day in the past when the Son of God gave himself for us, assuring us that we matter

117

profoundly to God, despite our sin. They are tokens of that precious moment in history when love took on a new meaning and depth. They invite us to remember and cherish—but above all, to be *reassured* of—the wonderful love of God for sinners like us.

Questions for discussion
- Can an atheist have doubts?
- Is God faithful to his promises?
- How can you reassure and remind yourself of God's love for you?

Doubt: how to handle it

Chapter 6

Doubt: how to handle it

The previous four chapters have dealt with specific doubts and anxieties that cause concern for many Christians. Since this work is aimed chiefly at students and young Christians, I have concentrated on doubts that often occur in the early stages of growth in faith. But doubt is something that is experienced by *all* Christians. In this chapter, we shall deal with some more general strategies for coping with doubt throughout the life of faith.

Faith and a hostile culture

In 1942 C. S. Lewis described faith as existing on "enemy territory." Writing during the Second World War, when much of continental Europe was occupied by Nazi armies, Lewis was trying to express the idea that faith was like a resistance movement that was hostile to the invading power. That invading power was determined to stamp out any resistance it met. Since World War II, Western culture has become much more aggressively secular. Those committed to secular values have a vested interest in destroying the credibility of the Christian faith—and that means *your* personal faith as well. It is very common for Christians to find themselves isolated at work, or ridiculed for their faith. They are very conscious of the fact that their faith marks them out as "abnormal" in the eyes of their colleagues. It's almost as if you have to apologize for believing in God. Christian values and presuppositions are gradually being squeezed out of every area of modern Western culture. "Christianity is a fighting religion" (C. S. Lewis). Faith, like a resistance movement, has to survive in a very hostile environment. But it *can* survive.

Many Christians find the new aggressiveness of secular culture deeply disturbing. It seems to call their faith into question. The hostility of much of modern Western society seems very threatening. It causes many Christians to become despondent. At best, the world seems indifferent to their faith; at worst, it treats it as absurd. Doubt can thus arise from a sense of bewilderment, of despondency at the hostility of the world (often including close friends and relatives) to the gospel. How can I believe the gospel when it meets such hostility and aggression?

There are three points to be made here, both academic and pastoral. But their underlying theme is the same. Modern Western culture is going through a phase that is not just non-Christian, but actually anti-Christian. That means you must be realistic about the hostile attitudes against Christianity that you are likely to encounter at every level. It has no bearing on whether Christianity is right or wrong. But it *does* place you under pressure because of your faith. So you must be realistic about the origin and purpose of this anti-Christian propaganda and learn to cope with it. With that in mind, let's look at these three points.

First, the popular reaction to an idea has no bearing on whether it is true or not. People may ridicule your faith in God—but that doesn't mean it is wrong. Most people have little understanding of what Christianity is all about. Very often, they reject a caricature of the gospel, not the gospel itself. You may well find that once you begin to *explain* what Christians believe (and why they believe it!), some of the hostility and lack of understanding begin to disappear. "We have got used to the fact that people make fun of things they don't understand" (Goethe). It isn't as if everyone has tried Christianity and decided it is no good. Nor is it as if they've all thought deeply about it and decided it can't be right. Most people give Christianity little thought and very often base even that on misunderstandings. You may find yourself in the privileged position of helping people come to faith by removing their misconceptions and misunderstandings of the gospel.

Second, try to project yourself into the situation faced by the first Christians during the New Testament period. They were faced with hostility on every side. They were ridiculed as fools (a very early anti-Christian graffito shows a kneeling man worshiping a crucified man who has the head of an ass). They were very few in number. There were enormous barriers of culture and language to overcome if the gospel was to be spread. Try to imagine yourself in their situation and how incredibly despondent you might feel about it! Yet the first Christians were not unduly worried by these problems. They weren't overwhelmed by the hostility of their environment. The resurrection of Jesus set those difficulties in perspective. The God who raised Jesus from the dead was with them and on their side. Like the first Christians, neither should we feel intimidated or threatened. In fact, the new hostility of secular culture to the gospel makes it easier for us to identify with the Christian communities we read about in the New Testament. In many respects, their situation is very like ours. So take comfort from the experience of the early Christians and let yourself be inspired and encouraged by their words and examples.

Third, appreciate the pastoral importance of support groups. Make sure you don't get isolated and have to cope with society's pressures on your own. You need to be encouraged by other Christians. You need to spend time with other people whose "worldview" is the same as yours. This is particularly important for Christian students at college or university where pressure from secular beliefs and values can be considerable. The world aims to isolate you, to demoralize you, to break down your confidence in yourself and the gospel (read John 17:14–18). You need to be able to discuss problems you have in common—such as how to cope with the pressure brought on Christians by society in general, by your colleagues at work, or by your family and friends in particular. Doubt can be a symptom of inadequate pastoral support. Don't just *go* to church— *get involved* in home groups, Bible study groups, special interest groups, or camps. Encourage your fellow Christians, and let them encourage you.

Don't get preoccupied with your doubts

Don't worry too much about doubt! Doubt focuses attention on yourself and your anxieties and keeps you from trusting in God. A preoccupation with doubt is just as pointless as a preoccupation with death: it doesn't change the situation, and it diverts your attention from the opportunities that the life of faith has to offer. Preoccupation with doubt is like constant spiritual introspection, in which you spend all your time looking inward at your own feelings and doubts when you should be looking outward to the living God who brought your faith into being and has promised to nourish and support that faith through the hard times. Preoccupation with doubt weakens or even cuts the lifeline between yourself and the living God; it distracts you from your life of prayer and devotion. This sort of pointless preoccupation with doubt paralyzes your spiritual growth. You stagnate because you lack motivation to grow.

Doubt is like an attention-seeking child: when you pay attention to it, it demands that you pay even more attention. You get locked into a vicious circle from which it is difficult to escape. If you feed your doubts, they'll grow! Yet doubt can bring home to us just how precious a thing faith is. It brings home to us how unthinkable life would be without the comforting presence of God. Doubt allows us to step briefly from the world of faith into the world of unbelief and realize how hostile and frightening a place it must be. The grass isn't always greener on the other side of the fence! So see doubt instead as an invitation to nourish your *faith* and deprive your doubts of the attention they need to grow.

125

Anyway, learn to see doubt *positively*. Don't be depressed by it, or let it get the upper hand. View it as an opportunity rather than as a problem. See it as an invitation to grow in faith and consolidate your spiritual resources rather than as a sign of decay. Your faith will decay only if you let doubt overwhelm you.

Doubt is also an invitation to spiritual growth because it can be a sign of a *neglected* faith—a faith that has been taken for granted and not nourished and allowed to grow. It points to a vulnerable faith. We need to work continually at all our relationships, consolidating and deepening them—and that applies to our relationship with God as well. Doubt is a sign that we've neglected our relationship with God. It's not the symptom that's important—it's the malaise it indicates. It's not the sign that's important—it's what it points to. Doubt signals the need for spiritual renewal, growth, and consolidation. So don't get preoccupied with your doubts: instead, get to work on renewing, deepening, and consolidating your faith in God. Just as an undernourished person is especially prone to illness, so a neglected and undernourished faith is particularly susceptible to doubt. Prevention, we are told, is better than cure—and this applies to doubt as much as to anything else.

It is therefore important to develop strategies that enable your faith to develop. That doesn't mean trying harder to believe: it means allowing your faith to rest on firmer personal and doctrinal foundations. We have already stressed the need to deepen your understanding of Christian doctrine: the more you understand your faith, the greater your confidence in its ideas. But what about the personal foundations of faith? What does it mean to develop the "personal foundations" of faith? An exposition of the parable of the sower will help make this important way of coping with doubt clearer.

The parable of the sower

One of the most positive ways of handling doubt is to read the parable of the sower (Mark 4:1–20), and reflect carefully on its implications. It is one of the most powerful parables, vividly conveying some important points. One of its main emphases is the goodness of the seed. Whatever happens to the seed is a result of the ground on which it falls; it does not reflect variable quality in the seed itself. As Jesus stresses, the seed represents the Word of God. The Word of God is able to effect the transformation of our lives. Just as the Word of God was able to call creation into existence (Genesis 1:1–27), so the same creative Word is able to transform our sinful lives, recreating us after the likeness of God.

But what if we present that seed with unsuitable soil? What if we, by the reception that we give to that seed, make it difficult for it to take root and grow? Doubt is a symptom of poor soil that has been neglected and starved of nutrients. The parable is an invitation to consider what sort of ground we are providing for the seed—can it grow and flourish? Existing doubt may be overcome, and future doubt made less likely, by allowing the seed of the gospel to grow vigorously in the ground of your life (Hosea 10:12). That ground needs to be tilled and made fertile—something that you can do. The consideration of two different kinds of seed helps bring this point out clearly.

The seed sown in rocky places (vv. 5–6; 16–17)

Here, the seed falls on rocky ground. This doesn't mean ground littered with rocks; rather, it means ground with a very thin layer of soil over the solid rock beneath. The seed is able to germinate without difficulty. However, when it tries to take root there is insufficient earth available. It is unable to develop a root that will enable it to gain access to water and necessary minerals, and to be physically stable. As a result, it cannot survive.

Some people develop a very superficial faith in the gospel that never takes root properly. Often it is very emotional in character, relying heavily on the experience of the presence of God or an unbalanced understanding of the work of the Holy Spirit. While such a faith is initially enormously enthusiastic it lacks real substance. It is like the house that was built on sand rather than rock—it lacks a solid foundation. Superficial faith is dependent on human emotional states rather than on the promises of God. As a result, this faith is very vulnerable to doubt. The moment God isn't *experienced* as present there is a temptation to assume he isn't present at all.

To change this situation, you need to replace this rocky ground with good soil so that the seed may take root. Stop relying on your emotions and feelings and let your faith feed upon the promises of God. It is very helpful to meditate on the promises of God (for example, in the Psalms), reflecting on their vitality and relevance. Find time to read books that will deepen your *understanding* of the Christian faith—in other words, books that will help you see how solid and substantial Christianity really is. You don't need to read very many, and you don't need to read them very quickly!

Much of the popular literature read by Christians is

biographical, about the lives and experiences of Christians. In many ways, of course, this is very helpful. It allows you to see how others have faced challenges similar to yours. It gives you some models for developing your own lifestyle as a Christian. It suggests things that you might not otherwise have thought about. And it's usually easy reading. Despite all these obvious advantages, a serious difficulty remains. Such books may tell you a lot about the people who wrote them, or the people who they're about—but they don't necessarily teach you much about *God*. They don't necessarily deepen your understanding of the Christian faith.

So spend time developing your understanding and knowledge of the Christian faith. It is by feeding your faith that you can starve your doubts to death. It is by letting your faith grow that your doubts will be choked. How? Some suggestions may prove helpful. Although they are particularly aimed at students, they are of relevance to a much wider audience.

1. Read Scripture regularly with a daily study plan. Note verses that seem helpful or relevant. Memorize them. Use a commentary to help you grasp the meaning of passages. And don't allow your study to be purely academic: your faith affects the way you act, your values and aspirations, as well as your ideas! Identify areas of your life in which you feel there is room for improvement in the light of your reading of Scripture, and especially your reflections on Jesus himself. Allow faith to become obedience. Allow your head and heart to interact!

And don't get permanently locked into a pattern of Bible reading or prayer that reflects the specific rhythm of student life! You must be prepared to be adaptable.

As a student, you may find that you can set aside a period early in the morning or late at night for Bible study and prayer. But what happens if you become a parent, and have small children who prevent you from getting a good night's sleep? What happens if you enter a career that makes severe demands at just those times you used to set aside for prayer? Be prepared to adapt. Develop new patterns of prayer—if necessary grabbing time as and when it arises. It is more important to read Scripture and pray than to do these things at a fixed time! Let your prayer pattern be realistic, tailored to your present situation—not to what things were like for you ten or twenty years ago!

2. Read some books that will stimulate your thinking about the content of your faith. This will not merely help you develop your own Christian mind—it will give you the resources to help others think through similar questions. One of the most helpful writers in this connection is C. S. Lewis, now widely regarded as probably the most important popular Christian writer of the twentieth century. *Mere Christianity*, *The Problem of Pain*, and *Miracles* are excellent works with which to begin thinking through a range of important questions. His collection *The Chronicles of Narnia*, especially *The Lion, The Witch and the Wardrobe*, presents many central Christian ideas in the form of a children's tale that has become a modern classic. You can cut your theological teeth on these, and enjoy yourself at the same time!

If you are experiencing doubt, you will find Lewis' *Screwtape Letters* particularly fascinating. In this book Lewis speculates on the strategies and tactics of a senior and a junior devil whose task it is to convert you to atheism! You will probably see doubt and temptation in a new light as a result. According to Lewis, doubt is something you must *expect* to happen. The stronger your faith, the more likely you are to be subjected to attack by doubt. Doubt is part of Screwtape's strategy for paralyzing and crippling your faith, and preventing you from being of some use to God. Doubt, like temptation, is something that Screwtape uses to distance you from God. If insights like this seem helpful, there are many more like them within the pages of *The Screwtape Letters*.

3. Read some books that will stimulate your thinking about prayer and Christian devotion. Remember that people have been putting their trust in Jesus Christ for the past two thousand years, and many have written of their experiences in works that have become spiritual classics. Many of these are easy to get hold of: by dipping in to them you can help yourself develop your prayer and devotional life. There are times when many Christians find prayer difficult, or feel that they are going through a spiritual dry spell—a period in which their spiritual life seems dry and parched (see Psalm 63:1; 143:6). If this is your problem, don't accept it passively—use it actively. Let God work through it. Reading classic works about prayer and devotion (an area often referred to as "spirituality") can help you through these difficult periods, as well as provide a great stimulus at other times.

Some examples may prove helpful. In 1418 a book entitled *The Imitation of Christ*, written by Thomas à Kempis, began to be read widely and soon became a classic. It is broken down into 114 short chapters, each usually less than a page long, rich in scriptural quotations and allusions. Each chapter deals with a single theme—for example, "On loving Jesus above all things," "On close friendship with Jesus," "On obedience, after the example of Christ," or "On asking God's help, and the certainty of his grace." Although written by a monk for monks, the book has freshness, profundity, and power that have stimulated generations of believers. It is a work into which you can dip occasionally or read regularly. As a sample, here are some of his thoughts on doubt, taken from the chapter "On resisting temptations":

> The beginning of all evil temptation is an unstable mind and lack of trust in God. Just as a ship without a helm is driven to and fro by the waves, so a careless man, who abandons his proper course, is tempted in countless ways. . . . So we must not despair when we are tempted, but earnestly pray to God to grant us his help in every need. For, as Paul says, "when you are tempted, God will provide a way to overcome it, so that we may be able to bear it." So let us humble ourselves under the hand of God in every trial and difficulty, for he will save and raise up the humble in spirit.

By dipping into works such as these, useful "thoughts for the day" can be gleaned. There are, of course, many other writers in addition to Thomas à Kempis—but he is an excellent starting point for those new to this type of writing. You might also like to try Brother Lawrence's *Practice of the Presence of God*. But remember that spirituality is largely a matter of personal taste! If you don't like a particular writer, try a different one.

4. Try keeping a spiritual diary in which you can jot down scripture references that seem helpful to your needs, or quotations from books that you have read that helped you think through a problem or that seemed to

cast light on some difficulty. You can just note page references to books if you find sections that seem relevant to your needs. Later, you can read through this book and benefit from your accumulated insights. We all know how very easy it is to forget precisely where a useful passage is to be found just when you need it most!

The seed sown among thorns (vv. 7, 18–19)

Some seed fell on ground in which there were other plants (thorns) already growing. If nothing more was done, there would have been intense competition for water, light, and space in which to grow. The problem is well-known to every gardener: before planting seed, first get rid of all the weeds! If you don't, they will choke the seed as it attempts to grow. The seed of the gospel *has* been planted in your life. It *is* already growing. But that growth can easily be threatened.

Try to imagine how a professional gardener goes about planting valuable seeds. He won't throw them on uncleared ground, where other plants can deprive them of the sunlight, warmth, and moisture essential to their germination and growth. He'll create the most favorable growing conditions he can, ensuring that nothing will get in the way of his valuable seeds. He will plant them in compost, free from other seeds or plants. He will ensure that they receive warmth, light, and adequate water.

God has already planted the seed of the gospel in your heart and mind. It is already growing. You can be assured of that. Now it's up to you to encourage its growth. This means uprooting thorns and other such plants that will prevent the seed of the gospel from growing properly. If this isn't done, the seed hasn't much of a chance. It will be choked by plants that are already there. Faith cannot grow in this situation and it will be exceptionally vulnerable to doubt. To allow faith to grow and develop its resistance to doubt, you must eliminate competition for your heart and mind. You must help it to grow by removing obstacles to that growth.

What sort of obstacles? The parable identifies several: the worries of this life, the lure of wealth, and the desire to possess other things (v. 19). Basic human ambition, the desire to be rich and famous, the thirst to outperform our competitors, anxieties about money and status—all these are competing for growing space with the gospel in our lives. To change the image slightly, they are competing for our *loyalty*. You cannot serve two masters, such as God and money (Matthew 6:24). This point is made with special clarity in 1 Timothy 6:8–10, which stresses the destructive effects of total dedication to the quest for money.

A faith under such pressure is very vulnerable to doubt. Anxieties about status, security, power, or money can easily encroach on our relationship with God. Jesus spoke powerfully of the effects of the cares and anxieties of the world on faith, and commended studying the birds of the air and the lilies of the field as an example of the tranquility of faith (Matthew 6:25–34). Note the constant stress: do not worry. Do not be anxious. Trust in God, and all else will fall into perspective. It is by seeking the kingdom of God and his righteousness—rather than worldly status or possessions—that peace of mind and growth in faith comes, bringing in their wake what we need for our daily life.

This section of the parable of the sower thus points to a definite course of action on our part. We are being asked to examine ourselves, to ask what our top priorities are. In examining yourself, it is very helpful to make a list of the matters uppermost in your mind at the moment, grading them in order of importance. "Where your heart is, there is your God also" (Martin Luther). For most of us, drawing up a list like this is a very revealing experience. It brings home to us how preoccupied we are with anxieties and concerns that have no direct bearing on our Christian life. If we do not look after our faith, can we be surprised if it falters occasionally? If we direct all our efforts toward other goals, we have correspondingly less time and inclination to work at our relationship with God. In fact, by concentrating our attention on matters relating to our status, wealth, and power, we are actually encouraging the growth of thorns that will choke the seed of the gospel (to use the imagery of the parable).

Doubt can therefore be a symptom of a neglected faith—a faith that has been untended and uncared for. Nevertheless, that neglect can be reversed. The thorn bushes that have up to now been choking faith can be removed, gradually or immediately. You can take steps to eliminate the anxieties that so often give rise to doubt. The first stage in this process is to identify these anxieties, next attempt to trace their causes, and finally correct your actions to eliminate anxieties. You can do this on your own, or in consultation with a friend or older Christian. What sort of anxieties are we talking about?

Try to answer this question yourself. Write on a sheet of paper the thoughts that are uppermost in your mind.

What thoughts are dominant at this moment? Who or what is at the top of your list of mental priorities? Most Christians, if they are being honest, find that God tends to be low on the list. Other matters assume greater importance. Drawing up this kind of list is an excellent way of recalling us to God because, to paraphrase Martin Luther, "where your heart is, there is also your God." In other words, whatever we give mental priority to *is* our God. What a frightening thought! Seeing our anxieties listed on paper thus helps us see what we treat as being really important, and shows us how easy it is to let God slip down our list of priorities.

Your faith *affects* your everyday life—but your faith is also *affected by* everyday life. Your faith isn't like some kind of watertight compartment insulated against everything else! What you believe about God affects the way you live—your hopes, your moral standards, and your general outlook on life. But this interaction is a two-way street. What's happening to you in your everyday life affects the quality of your faith. If you are depressed about your career or your family, if a relationship is going wrong, or if you are worried about money—then don't be surprised if these anxieties reduce your spiritual well-being.

For most people, the types of anxiety that can give rise to doubt are far more mundane than those that arise from the worlds of power politics and high finance. Let's look at some obvious examples. Again, although they focus on student concerns, they apply equally well to other situations.

1. Personal relationships. For two people involved in a personal relationship one person may become a Christian while the other does not. This can cause

enormous difficulties and tensions. In the first place, becoming a Christian involves a new interest in God that expresses itself in certain very obvious ways—a new interest in reading the Bible, talking about Jesus Christ, going to church, getting involved with Christian groups, and so forth. This change can be very distressing for the other person, who is probably unable to understand what has happened, let alone share in it. In the second place, it means becoming involved with a new group of people—at church, at the college or campus Christian union, or at a local home group. The other party feels excluded from these.

It is very difficult for someone who has just become a Christian to avoid feeling the tension this change has created within the personal relationship, and as a result they become prone to anxiety and distress. In fact, sadly, it is quite common for the relationship to break up. The tension within this relationship, while it lasts (that is, either the tension or the relationship itself), is like a thornbush that can seriously interfere with the growth of faith and the development of Christian maturity. If you are in such a position concerning a relationship, and find doubt a problem, it is advisable to attempt to resolve the difficulties within that relationship (for example, by sharing your newfound faith and what it means to you). Perhaps the other party will feel able to accept your position and may even eventually come to share it. However, it is necessary to inject a note of somber realism into this discussion by pointing out that the more usual course is for the relationship to break up. So, a simple word of advice: let your serious relationships be with other Christians!

At this stage most student relationships are of an

exploratory nature, not necessarily leading to permanence as in marriage. The trauma caused by the breakup of such a relationship is thus not as severe as it might otherwise be. This difficulty is much more serious, of course, within a marriage when one of the partners comes to faith and the other remains in a state of unbelief. The tensions that this can create are considerable, and require handling with sensitivity and compassion. While a detailed response to this difficulty is impossible within the limited space of this work, the suggestions for further reading on practical problems that spill over into the spiritual life at the end of the book should prove helpful in coping with and perhaps resolving such a situation.

2. Work. Some students find themselves seriously behind with their work due to illness, a fundamental inability to cope with their subject, laziness, or a lack of personal discipline. The pressure that work can create is considerable and may totally dominate a student's horizons. As a result of this pressure, a student can easily become swamped with work and be thrown into a state of despair.

All his or her resources are drawn into the struggle to keep up with essay deadlines or topic assignments, with everything else being neglected in order to focus on this one objective. It is hardly surprising that God tends to get squeezed out of such situations. If this is happening to you, it is important to realize what is going on. There are ways of coping with work and the stress that it causes. You can explore those ways through the material suggested for further reading: investigate these!

Problems with work often arise from sheer laziness or a lack of personal discipline. These are weaknesses that can also affect your faith. If you lack discipline in work, you will probably also lack discipline in prayer and studying Scripture. If you take a laid-back attitude to your work, you will probably also take the same attitude to your faith. The result is a vulnerable and superficial faith. Why not aim for a sense of personal discipline in both your work and your faith?

3. Anxiety about the future. It is perfectly understandable that you should be anxious about the future, especially during your final year at college or university. The decisions that you make can be of considerable importance in affecting your future career, as well as have enormous implications for the remainder of your life. Some students feel overwhelmed by such anxieties, once more making them vulnerable to doubt. It is important that you commit such decisions to God. Ask him for guidance, for wisdom, and for courage to make the right decisions. But above all, ask for peace of mind as you explore possibilities for the future. The Old Testament word for faith can be translated as "being strong in the Lord": learn to trust in him, to commit the unknown future to the known care of the Lord. See yourself as being like Abraham or Joshua, setting out into the unknown future, secure in the knowledge that, wherever they went and whatever happened to them, the Lord would be with them by their side (Genesis 12:1–2; Joshua 1:1–9). There is much material available on vocational guidance that you might find helpful; you will find some suggestions at the end of this chapter.

These, then, are some of the ways in which faith can be weakened through outside factors. Remember this if you feel low or depressed and far from God. You are not immune from outside influences—in fact, all of us are highly vulnerable to them. Try to identify what it is that is making you feel anxious and see if you can do something about it. Try to develop a sense of spiritual discipline, as suggested below, and not be unduly influenced by your circumstances.

Develop spiritual discipline

Many Christians draw back from the idea of spiritual discipline. They may suspect that it is inconsistent with the freedom of the gospel. They may view it as a lapse into some form of legalism. Actually, it's nothing of the sort. It is a means by which God may graciously deepen our faith in him, our knowledge of him, and our obedience to him. It means taking God seriously enough to try and ensure we get to spend time with him despite all the pressures on us. It means acknowledging that we cannot hope to keep going as Christians without the continual support of God. It means structuring our lives to allow that support to get through. This is not legalism, a routine for a routine's sake: rather, it is a sign of the deepening obedience and commitment that are the hallmarks of a maturing faith.

Suppose you take up a demanding job in a major international corporation, or in a caring agency in which considerable demands are made of your time and attention. It is very easy to become so busy, so preoccupied with countless matters, that it becomes difficult to find time to spend with God. Everything else seems to get in the way. Many professionals look back with envy at their time as students, wishing that they had as much spare time now as they had then! Developing a spiritual discipline means setting aside time *as a matter of deliberate policy* to be with God.

140

If you're going through a spiritual dry spell and are finding the going rough, all the pressures of work or family that come to bear on you will make it difficult for you to find time to be alone with God. Yet your growth in faith depends on being able to spend time in this way. And if you aren't able to spend time with God in prayer and adoration you'll find that your faith becomes vulnerable. When you're under pressure you won't have access to the spiritual resources that will enable you to cope. Give yourself a break by allowing God space to draw alongside you.

By developing spiritual discipline, you can build time into your routine to be set aside for God. If you can start developing a discipline like this as a student, you'll find that it will stay with you afterward. What time of day should you set aside? Some prefer to set aside time early in the morning, before the day's work begins. It allows you time to commit the coming day to God, and ask for his strength and guidance to face all that it will bring. Some people find it helpful to pray with their diaries open in front of them. For others, the best time is late at night, when the pressures of the day are lifted. The day's work is over, the children are asleep, the world is quiet: you can spend time reading, meditating, and praying in peace. And try to keep Sunday special, despite all the pressure to work right through the weekend. If you're too busy to spend time with God, you're busier than God ever meant you to be.

The worst thing you can do in the event of a spiritual dry spell is to give up going to church, spending time with Christian friends and colleagues, or reading Scripture. These can keep you going when your prayer life seems to dry up. They are like roots, searching for precious moisture in a dry land. Jeremiah likened someone who trusts in the Lord to a tree planted by a stream (Jeremiah 17:7–8):

> Blessed is the man who trusts in the Lord, whose confidence is in him. He will be like a tree planted by the water that sends out its roots by the stream. It does not fear when heat comes; its leaves are always green. It has no worries in a year of drought and never fails to bear fruit.

So, keep your roots in place, waiting for the water to return—and return it will. "Wait for the Lord; be strong and take heart and wait for the Lord" (Psalm 27:14).

Let's look at the way spiritual discipline can help you handle doubt. In the first place, it helps make your faith less vulnerable. It builds time for reading Scripture, for praying, for waiting on God, into what can become an unbearably busy timetable. It ensures that you aren't cut off from your lifeline to God. It gives you access to vital spiritual resources that you will need to cope with the pressures of life.

When I studied biology at school, I remember learning about the water spider. This little spider lives on the bottom of ponds, in a small, thimble-like gossamer case. This case has a hole at its base, through which the spider can enter. On the surface of the pond, the spider entraps air bubbles by means of hooked hairs. He then dives down to the case and sets the air bubbles free inside the case. After several such trips, the spider has accumulated enough air to allow him to live in his case for some time beneath the water. Even though the environment is alien and hostile, the spider can survive—because of his air supply. However, eventually the oxygen in that vital air supply is used up. The spider is then obliged to return to the surface and gather more air. Without it, he cannot survive beneath the surface of the water.

As Christians we are in a situation similar to that water spider. We exist in a hostile environment, nourished and supported by resources from above. But our resources must be renewed and replenished—otherwise, they will run out. The spiritual life demands continual access to spiritual resources. The spider's regular journeys to the surface for air remind us of our need for regular fellowship with God, in order that our batteries may be recharged and our resources renewed (to jumble together several helpful images). We cannot allow those resources to become dangerously low: we do not know when we may need to draw heavily upon them. Just as the foolish maidens allowed the oil supplies in their lamps to grow dangerously low (Matthew 25:1–13), obliging them to miss the opportunity of greeting the bridegroom, so we must be disciplined in maintaining our spiritual resources. We never know when we might need them—and need them badly.

In the second place, it prevents you from burning your bridges (usually by accident, rather than by design), if you do go through a period of doubt. Younger Christians, in particular, are tempted to give up praying and reading Scripture if they stop experiencing the presence of God in their lives. Not only can experience be an unreliable guide to the reality and presence of God—by overreacting in this way, but you make it more difficult for God to draw you close to himself again. The sense of expectation of God is lost. At the first sign of doubt some young Christians panic and abandon their faith—needlessly. Soldiers learn discipline so that they

143

will not panic at the first sight of a threat. If you have developed a sense of spiritual discipline, you will reap the rewards of patience. Christianity is not an easy ride through life, but is a struggle against sin, disobedience, and doubt, all of which attempt to tear us away from God. It is a battle in which discipline adds strength to your own spiritual resources and allows you to draw increasingly upon the might of God.

These, then, are some strategies both for coping with doubt and for making your faith less vulnerable. Remember that a superficial faith is a vulnerable faith, just as a shallow-rooted plant is easily uprooted. In bringing this work to a close, however, it is proper to look more closely at doubt itself. In earlier chapters, we saw how doubt arose through not fully understanding the situation. The classic examples of this situation are provided by the Exodus of Israel from Egypt and by the crucifixion of Jesus Christ itself. Meditating on the Exodus and the death of Christ puts doubt in its proper perspective. Let's see how.

Doubt in perspective—the Exodus from Egypt

The Exodus from Egypt is one of the most powerful and memorable stories the world has ever known. It tells of the liberation of the people of Israel from their bondage in Egypt. It recounts their long and difficult struggle to gain access to the Promised Land. But it also helps us understand how doubt arises, and gives us some clues about how to see it in its proper perspective. Three points are of special importance.

It means leaving behind security. "Why did we ever leave Egypt? Things weren't so bad there!" For some of the Israelites, the realities of life as they passed from

144

Egypt to the Promised Land were unacceptable (e.g., Numbers 11:1–20). They began to look back on their days in Egypt with something approaching nostalgia! They thought that liberation from Egyptian captivity would mean the end of all their problems. Instead, they found themselves with a new set of problems!

Some people begin the Christian life with the mistaken idea that all will be marvelous thereafter. When things get tough, they begin to doubt. Yet what we are promised in the gospel is not an easy ride through life. The Christian life is difficult and demanding. Liberation from bondage to sin and the fear of death opens up the prospect of a new life—but they are not *easy* options. Our responsibilities to God are demanding, and the challenges he lays before us are considerable. But we are promised that, whatever life may hold for us, God will be present to support and sustain us. I simply cannot express adequately how comforting and important that is.

It means going through a wilderness period. The people of Israel set out from Egypt in good spirits. The presence and the power of God was made clear and real through signs and wonders. God seemed very close and very real during those first days. And then the long, hard journey through the wilderness began. The going got tough. The memory of the presence and power of God faded. Signs and wonders seemed far away. Disbelief and doubt began to set in. Of course, the promise of the presence of God had not been canceled. Nor had the Promised Land been set to one side. But the promises seemed unreal in the wilderness situation.

Some Christians encounter the same kind of experience. They feel that they are struggling through a spiritual wilderness. The dynamism and excitement they may have felt in the first days of faith seem to have gone forever. They are suffering from spiritual drought and famine and are unable to satisfy their needs. Doubt sets in. It is at this point that spiritual discipline becomes crucially important. Keep going! Learn to make the use of the resources available in that situation. After all, the Israelites were given manna from heaven to keep them going through the wilderness until they entered the Promised Land.

Look around and see what the Lord has made available to you. There are individuals you can talk to who have been through that same wilderness experience and can tell of its trials and tribulations. They can tell of the joy of leaving it behind, and of the spiritual lessons they learned. There are books that you can read. But above all, see a wilderness experience as a possible time of growth—a time in which you can learn more about yourself, and about God. A wilderness experience is a time of trial. Your faith is being tested, and its weak points identified to you.

An illustration may help make this clearer. I was born in Belfast, the capital city of Northern Ireland. One of the greatest moments in the history of that city was the launching of the White Star Liner *Titanic* in 1911. It was the greatest ship ever built, and it was designed to work the dangerous run across the Atlantic Ocean. But would it stand up to the conditions of that run? Would it survive the dangerous seas and the ice packs off the Canadian coast? In the course of its journeys across the ocean it would encounter severe and testing conditions. Could it cope with them?

To answer this question, the *Titanic* was subjected to

sea trials. In theory, sea trials would test the ship to its limits and show up any obvious weaknesses. Once these weaknesses were revealed they could be put right. Then the really dangerous voyages could be undertaken. Sadly, those sea trials were not severe enough. The ship passed as seaworthy. The cruel truth came to light when she sank on her maiden voyage in 1912 with terrible loss of life.

The Christian life is like a long and dangerous voyage during which your resources may be tested to the full on occasion. But will they be good enough? Is your faith deep enough and your trust in God strong enough? Think of doubt as being like a sea trial, gently showing up your weaknesses. Once you know what they are, you can do something about them—so that if real difficulties come your way, you'll be able to cope with them. It's all part of growing deeper in your faith (see 1 Corinthians 10:13; 1 Peter 5:10).

Doubt, then, can be a wilderness experience. If you feel you are going through this kind of experience, use it positively. Remember that Jesus himself went through a period of testing in the wilderness as God prepared him for the great tasks awaiting him (Matthew 4:1–11). Are you being prepared for a task? The early Christians used to go into the wilderness to get away from all sources of distraction so that they could concentrate upon God. Tell God about your feelings of doubt, of loneliness or emptiness. Commit them to him. And stay close to him. Trust him. The promised land is still there, awaiting your entry—with God by your side.

It means trusting in the promises of God. God promised the people of Israel "a land flowing with milk and honey" (Exodus 13:5). Yet during their period of

147

wandering in the wilderness they knew nothing but a barren land. The Promised Land was something held out in front of them like a carrot in front of a donkey. The thought kept them going. However, some found it too distant a hope. It was too far in the future. They wanted instant satisfaction. They had left behind security and the comfort of the known and were being asked to keep going into the unknown on the promises of God. For some that seemed too great a risk to take. And so they doubted.

Looking back on this, we can see that they were mistaken. The final entry into the Promised Land triumphantly vindicated the faithfulness of God to his promises. But you can understand their feelings at the time. The Promised Land seemed hopelessly distant. And for some Christians, the promises of eternal life seem very far off. If this is the case for you, try to think yourself into the Exodus situation. Try to imagine how difficult it must have been to trust in the promise of the land flowing with milk and honey when all around you was nothing but wilderness. Then turn your mind to that great moment when Israel crossed the Jordan and entered into the Promised Land. Can you see how the Exodus gives us insights into our own situation? It reminds us that, even though God's promises seem far off and distant, they will still be fulfilled. And we are not left without comfort as we trust: God gives us his Holy Spirit to comfort, reassure and challenge us as we journey in faith.

Doubt in perspective—the first Good Friday

Imagine what it was like for the disciples the first Good Friday. They had given up everything to follow

Jesus. Their whole reason for living centered on him. He seemed to have the answers to all their questions. Then, in front of their eyes, he was taken from them. He was to be publicly executed. You can feel an immense sense of despair as you read the gospel accounts of the death of Jesus. Perhaps the disciples were hoping for a miracle. Certainly, there were those in the crowd of spectators who expected God to intervene. Others were more skeptical. "He trusts in God. Let God rescue him now if he wants him" (Matthew 27:43). There seemed to be no trace of God's presence or activity at Calvary. As Jesus became weaker, the disciples must have become increasingly despondent. There was no sign of God intervening to transform the situation.

Finally, Jesus died. That was probably the darkest moment in the lives of the disciples. They were already demoralized enough, as Peter's denial of Jesus demonstrated. Now, as they watched the scene from a distance, it must have seemed as if their entire world had collapsed, shown up as a fraud and an illusion. What sorts of thoughts might have gone through their minds? Perhaps that Jesus was no different than any other man? Perhaps that God was not there—or that if he was, he showed no interest whatsoever in the fate of Jesus?

Of course, we know the outcome of that story. We know how the disciples' sorrow was transformed to joy and wonder as the news of the resurrection of Jesus became known. The theme of the resurrection of the crucified Christ pervades the writings of Paul, and provides the standpoint from which he interprets the crucifixion. The cross is not to be seen as a dead end, but as a crucial stage on the road to resurrection and glorification. When we read the gospel accounts of the

149

suffering and death of Jesus, we cannot help but think ahead to his resurrection. We know that there is a happy ending to this apparent tragedy.

Now try to imagine yourself standing among the disciples as they watched Jesus suffer and die—*without* knowing that he would be raised again from the dead. Set aside your knowledge of what happens later, and try to imagine what it must have been like to watch Jesus die on the cross. His suffering seemed utterly pointless. What could be achieved through it? And where was God in all this? Why didn't he intervene? It was all enough to make anyone doubt whether God existed in the first place. And if he *did* exist, he seemed to be totally indifferent to the sufferings of Jesus. What hope was there for anyone else if God treated Jesus in this way? It is easy to get a feel for the sense of despair and bewilderment on that sad day.

All those doubts were resolved through the resurrection. The apparently pointless suffering of Jesus was revealed as the means through which God was working out the salvation of sinful humanity. God was not absent from that scene; he was working to transform it from a scene of hopelessness and helplessness to one of joy and hope. God's love was *demonstrated*, not contradicted, by the death of his son (John 3:16; Romans 5:8). The resurrection transformed the disciple's understanding of the way in which God was present and active in his world.

Let's apply this model and see what insights it affords. First, it brings home to us how unreliable experience and feelings can be as guides to the presence of God. Those around the cross didn't experience the presence of God—so they concluded that he was absent from the scene. The resurrection overturns that judgment: God was present in a hidden manner, which people mistook for his absence. Do you feel that God is absent from your life, or from certain difficult situations? Are you bewildered by events, or in despair over the way things are going? Then think of the first Good Friday, when God also seemed to be absent, only to be shown to have been working in a hidden and mysterious way to transform it in a totally unexpected manner. The promise of resurrection was there: Jesus had assured his disciples that he would be raised to life on the third day after his crucifixion (Matthew 20:17–19). Yet, in the desperation of that crucial moment, that promise had been forgotten, perhaps doubted. Experience seemed to suggest it could not be fulfilled. The first Good Friday reminds us of the need to trust in the divine promises, rather than rely on our feelings and experience.

Second, it allows us insights into the mystery of human suffering. Without knowledge of the resurrection, the sufferings of Christ seemed pointless and meaningless. With the knowledge of the resurrection, and the inestimable benefits of salvation and forgiveness that flow from it, those sufferings are seen in a new light. He suffered for us so that through his suffering our sin might be forgiven and our human natures healed. "He took up our infirmities and carried our sorrows...he was pierced for our transgressions" (Isaiah 53:4–5).

This theme is developed in many ways in the New Testament. Perhaps its bearing on the suffering of believers is of most relevance to this discussion. For Paul, Christians are those who are heirs of God by adoption (Ephesians 1:4–5; cf. Romans 8:12–21). They are entitled to receive from God the same inheritance as his own son, Jesus Christ. What is that inheritance? As the cross and resurrection make clear, the inheritance of the believer is glory gained through suffering. "We share in his sufferings in order that we may also share in his glory" (Romans 8:17). Suffering is thus seen as a sign of faith, a token of the glory that is to come. It is not something that can be bypassed.

Thinking of the first Good Friday, then, helps us put our doubt in context. It allows us to see it in a new and proper perspective. We learn to see our own situation, our own doubts, our own anxieties, as being like that scene at Calvary. People asked questions that could not be answered; they voiced doubts that could not be silenced. It seemed difficult to trust God. Yet those questions and doubts were seen in a new light because of the resurrection of Jesus Christ. God surprised everybody on that first Easter Day. It is this model that provides a key to our own questions, doubts, and anxieties.

Doubt arises partly because of our inability to see the whole picture, to understand how the various elements of our experience interlock. Just as faith sees the crucifixion in terms of the resurrection, so we must view the perplexities of the world in the light of its future transformation into the New Jerusalem (Revelation 21:1–5). The hopelessness and helplessness of Good Friday are given new meaning in the light of Easter Day, just as the ambiguities and suffering of the present day will be seen in a new light when God brings history to its end. Good Friday and Easter Day are models for understanding the way God is present in and at work in his world: just as Good Friday is given its meaning through Easter Day, so the pain and problems of the present day will be given new meaning at the end of time. The doubt of Good Friday gives way to the faith of Easter Day. We do not fully understand how God is working out his purposes for the world and for us; what we do know is that God affirms, in word and in deed, his utter faithfulness to us. He is one in whom we can trust. "Cast all your anxiety on him, because he cares for you" (1 Peter 5:7). If we cannot trust God, who can we trust?

Perhaps some will suggest we should rely on our own perception of the situation, which seems to raise difficulties for faith. But, as the events of Calvary indicate, our perceptions of the situation can be hopelessly misleading and inaccurate: it is at best a *partial* perception, in that we do not have access to all the data we need in order to make an informed analysis of the situation. God was perceived to be absent from the crucifixion—until the resurrection demonstrated him to have been present, secretly working out the redemption of humanity and the glorification of his son.

Perhaps others might suggest that we rely on our feelings and emotions. If God isn't *felt* as real, he *isn't* real, they might suggest. If we don't *experience* him as present, he *isn't* present. But how unreliable our feelings can be here! They are influenced by a huge variety of factors: our health, the weather, the state of our bank balance, our personal relationships, our work or career—just to name the more obvious ones! God doesn't cease to exist just because you've had a bad day at the office or had an argument with a friend. Your emotions, distracted and confused by your various anxieties, may tell you that God isn't there—but that is not a particularly reliable or informed judgment!

In the end, Christianity stands or falls with the trustworthiness and reliability of the God who raised Jesus Christ from the dead. By meditating on that first Good Friday, we can remind ourselves of the unreliability of our own judgment on the one hand, and the faithfulness of God to his promises on the other—and thus we can put doubt in its proper perspective. For, seen properly, doubt is not a threat to faith, but a reminder of how fragile a hold we have on our knowledge of God, and how gracious God is in having revealed himself to us. For, without God's revelation of himself we would have been left totally in the dark concerning him and his love for us. God is not capricious or whimsical, nor does he fail to stand by his promises or to act in accordance with his nature and character as we know it through Scripture and through Jesus Christ. Instead, we know a God who is faithful to his covenant, who promises mercy and forgiveness to those who put their trust in him. Instead of trusting in our own perception of a situation, or relying on our feelings and emotions, we should learn to trust in the faithfulness and constancy of God.

Conclusion

Doubt is a subject that many Christians find both difficult and sensitive. They may see it as something shameful and disloyal, on the same level as heresy. As a result, it is often something that they don't—or won't — talk about. They suppress it. Others fall into the opposite trap—they get totally preoccupied with doubt. They get overwhelmed. They lose sight of God through concentrating upon themselves. Yet doubt is something too important to be treated in either of these ways.

Viewed positively, doubt provides opportunities for spiritual growth. It tests your faith and shows you where it is vulnerable. It forces you to think about your faith, and not just take it for granted. It stimulates you to strengthen the foundations of your relationship with God.

I hope that this book will not just help you to handle doubts, but will allow you to begin evolving strategies for spiritual discipline and growth, developing both the personal and doctrinal aspects of your faith. Viewed positively, doubt can be a way to rediscovering the full depths of faith and of growing in your commitment to the gospel. "The one who calls you is faithful and he will do it" (1 Thessalonians 5:24).

Questions for discussion

- In what ways can you reinforce your faith against doubt?
- Why is a superficial faith so vulnerable to doubt?
- Is doubt insulting to God?
- What books have you and your friends found helpful in deepening your faith?
- In what ways are the following helpful in countering doubt: fellowship, praise, discipline, understanding?

For further reading

On the nature of doubt:

Os Guinness, *Doubt.* A detailed examination of the nature of doubt with helpful exploration of its origins. Difficult to read, but worth the effort for those able to cope with it.

On developing your understanding of your faith:

Alister McGrath, *Explaining Your Faith.* A useful guide through some of the areas of the Christian faith that cause difficulties for some people. This work will allow you to deepen your own understanding of your faith, while at the same time preparing you to explain it to others.

John R. W. Stott, *Basic Christianity.* A concise and neat summary of the main points of the Christian faith, carefully explained and justified. Ideal for helping you think through your faith.

On dealing with specific problem areas of faith:

F. F. Bruce, *The Real Jesus.* Useful material for those who wonder whether Christianity has got Jesus wrong.

R. T. France, *The Evidence for Jesus.* An impressive historical survey of the historical evidence for the existence of Jesus.

E. M. B. Green, *The Empty Cross of Jesus.* A splendid study of the evidence for the resurrection of Jesus and its implications for the way in which we think and live.

C. S. Lewis, *Mere Christianity.* Perhaps the best justification of Christian belief generally available.

C. S. Lewis, *Miracles.* A superb defense of miracles with many helpful comments on various aspects of the Christian faith.

C. S. Lewis, *The Problem of Pain*. One of the most widely read works on the theme of pain and suffering.

C. S. Lewis, *The Screwtape Letters*. A "behind the scenes" account of doubt and temptation, written with wit and insight.

Alister McGrath, *Understanding Jesus*. A readable and comprehensive account of the importance of Jesus for the Christian faith.

Alister McGrath, *Understanding the Trinity*. Essential reading for those puzzled by the doctrine of the Trinity, with useful material on the existence of God.

J. R. W. Stott, *The Cross of Christ*. A splendid account of the meaning of the cross for Christian faith.

Andrew Walker, *Enemy Territory*. An excellent discussion of the strongly anti-Christian character of modern Western culture.

Philip Yancey, *Disappointment With God*. Thoughtful discussion of a wide range of doubts frequently encountered by Christians and non-Christians.

On developing spiritual discipline:

Allan Coppedge, *Biblical Principles of Discipleship*. Useful guide to the discipling process, with emphasis on the need for commitment.

Wesley L. Duewel, *Touch the World Through Prayer*. This work discusses every aspect of prayer from those for whom you can pray to how to pray with power to organizing your prayer life.

Richard Foster, *Celebration of Discipline*. This work is full of good ideas about deepening your knowledge and love of God. It also includes helpful lists for further reading, including some of the great spiritual classics.

Peter Gillquist, *The Physical Side of Being Spiritual*. Stimulating work packed with insights on worship and spiritual discipline.

Thomas à Kempis, *The Imitation of Christ*. A classic devotional study, well worth dipping into.

Kenneth Cain Kinghorn, *Discovering Your Spiritual Gifts*. A personal inventory method for identifying your gifts, which many have found helpful.

Ronald Klug, *How to Keep a Spiritual Journal*. Useful advice on building up a personal notebook of faith as a spiritual resource.

Brother Lawrence, *The Practice of the Presence of God*. A fine guide to deepening your devotional life.

Richard Lovelace, *Dynamics of Spiritual Life*. A comprehensive history of spiritual renewal, likely to stimulate your own thinking on this matter.

Gordon MacDonald, *Restoring Your Spiritual Passion*. Helpful guide for those who feel that their faith is tired and weary.

Gordon MacDonald, *Ordering Your Private World*. Practical advice and useful insights on sorting out difficulties that interfere with spiritual development.

Lawrence O. Richards, *A Practical Theology of Spirituality*. Useful theoretical grounding in the field of spiritual discipline.

On practical problems that spill over into the spiritual life:

Jack Dominian, *Marriage, Faith and Love*. Especially helpful for those who find themselves coming to faith within marriage.

Jacques Ellul, *Money and Power*. Recommended for those worried about the relation of faith and wealth, or who find themselves preoccupied with money. Particularly helpful on the idea of "mammon."

Calvin Redekop and Urie A. Bender, *Who am I? What am I?* An invaluable guide to the Christian's attitude to work.

Denny Rydberg, *How to Survive in College*. Useful for the Christian college student trying to cope with a new environment and new pressures.

Denny Rydberg, *Beyond Graduation*. Thoughtful advice on coping with work and relationships after college.

Derek Tidball, *Skillful Shepherds*, pp. 249–65. A very helpful discussion of some pastoral aspects of faith and doubt, with special reference to contemporary culture.

Paul Tournier, *Marriage Difficulties*. Valuable on dealing with marriage partners who do not share your faith.

Bibliography

F. F. Bruce, *The Real Jesus*. Downers Grove, Ill.: InterVarsity Press, 1985.

Allan Coppedge, *The Biblical Principles of Discipleship*. Grand Rapids: Zondervan, 1989.

Jack Dominian, *Marriage, Faith and Love*. Darton, Longman and Todd, 1981.

Jacques Ellul, *Money and Power*. Downers Grove, Ill.: InterVarsity Press, 1984.

Richard Foster, *Celebration of Discipline*. San Francisco: Harper & Row, study edition, 1989.

R. T. France, *The Evidence for Jesus*. Downers Grove, Ill.: InterVarsity Press, 1986.

Peter Gillquist, *The Physical Side of Being Spiritual*. Grand Rapids: Zondervan, 1979.

E. M. B. Green, *The Empty Cross of Jesus*. Downers Grove, Ill.: InterVarsity Press, 1984.

Os Guinness, *Doubt: Faith in Two Minds*. Downers Grove, Ill.: InterVarsity Press, 1979.

Thomas à Kempis, *The Imitation of Christ*. Translated by E. M. Blaiklock. London: Hodder & Stoughton, 1982.

Kenneth Cain Kinghorn, *Discovering Your Spiritual Gifts*. Grand Rapids: Zondervan, 1987.

Ronald Klug, *How to Keep a Spiritual Journal*. New York: Nelson, 1982.

Brother Lawrence, *The Practice of the Presence of God*. Translated by E. M. Blaiklock. London: Hodder & Stoughton, 1982.

C. S. Lewis, *Mere Christianity*. New York: Macmillan, 1952.

C. S. Lewis, *Miracles*. New York: Macmillan, 1947.

C. S. Lewis, *The Problem of Pain*. New York: Macmillan, 1943.

C. S. Lewis, *The Screwtape Letters*. New York: Macmillan, 1962.

Richard Lovelace, *Dynamics of the Spiritual Life: An Evangelical Theology of Renewal*. Downers Grove, Ill.: InterVarsity Press, 1979.

Gordon MacDonald, *Restoring Your Spiritual Passion*. New York: Nelson, 1986.

Gordon MacDonald, *Ordering Your Private World*. New York: Nelson, 1984.

Alister McGrath, *Understanding Jesus: Who Jesus Christ Is and Why He Matters*. Grand Rapids: Zondervan, 1987.

Alister McGrath, *Understanding the Trinity*. Grand Rapids: Zondervan, 1988.

Alister McGrath, *Explaining Your Faith Without Losing Your Friends*. Grand Rapids: Zondervan, 1988.

Lawrence O. Richards, *A Practical Theology of Spirituality*. Grand Rapids: Zondervan, 1988.

Calvin Redekop and Urie A. Bender, *Who am I? What am I? Searching for Meaning in Your Work*. Grand Rapids: Zondervan, 1988.

Denny Rydberg, *How to Survive in College*. Grand Rapids: Zondervan, 1989.

Denny Rydberg, *Beyond Graduation*. Grand Rapids: Zondervan, 1988.

J. R. W. Stott, *The Cross of Christ*. Downers Grove, Ill.: InterVarsity Press, 1986.

J. R. W. Stott, *Basic Christianity*. Downers Grove, Ill.: InterVarsity Press, many reprints.

Derek Tidball, *Skillful Shepherds: An Introduction to Pastoral Theology*. Grand Rapids: Zondervan, 1988.

Paul Tournier, *Marriage Difficulties*. Crowborough: Highland Books, 1967.

Andrew Walker, *Enemy Territory: The Christian Struggle for the Modern World*. Grand Rapids: Zondervan, 1988.

Philip Yancey, *Disappointment With God*. Grand Rapids: Zondervan, 1988.